Retold Myths & Folktales

African Myths

African American Folktales

Asian Myths

Classic Myths, Volume 1

Classic Myths, Volume 2

Classic Myths, Volume 3

Mexican American Folktales

Native American Myths

Northern European Myths

World Myths

The Retold Tales® Series features novels, short story anthologies, and collections of myths and folktales.

Perfection Learning®

Writer

Jim Uhls
Playwright and Fiction Writer

Retold Myths & Folktales

CLASSIC MYTHS

VOLUME 3

Perfection Learning®

Editor in Chief
Kathleen Myers

Managing Editor
Beth Obermiller

Senior Editor
Marsha James

Editors
Kathie O'Sell
Christine Rempe LePorte

Cover Illustration
Michael Aspengren

Inside Illustration
Sam Van Meter

Book Design
Dea Marks

For information contact
Perfection Learning® Corporation
1000 North Second Avenue, P.O. Box 500
Logan, Iowa 51546-0500
Phone: 1-800-831-4190 • Fax: 1-800-543-2745
perfectionlearning.com

PB ISBN-13: 978-1-5631-2230-9 ISBN-10: 1-5631-2230-8
RLB ISBN-13: 978-0-7807-1664-3 ISBN-10: 0-7807-1664-7

16 17 18 19 20 PP 13 12 11 10 09 08

TABLE
OF CONTETS

WELCOME TO THE RETOLD CLASSIC MYTHS

You see the references everywhere. Look at great artwork like the *Venus de Milo*. Or classic literature such as James Joyce's *Ulysses*. Then think about our language, which is filled with words like *typhoon* and *panic*. You can even see them in ads for FTD Florist and Atlas moving company.

What do all these things, from art to ads, have in common? They're based on Greek and Roman classic myths.

We call something classic when it is so well loved that it is saved and passed down to new generations. Classics have been around for a long time, but they're not dusty or out of date. That's because they are brought back to life by each new person who sees and enjoys them.

The *Retold Classic Myths* are stories written years ago that continue to entertain or influence today. The tales offer exciting plots, important themes, fascinating characters, and powerful language. They are stories that many people have loved to hear and share with one another.

RETOLD UPDATE

This book presents a collection of eight adapted classics. All the colorful, gripping, comic details of the older versions are here. But in the Retold versions of the stories, long sentences and paragraphs have been split up.

In addition, a word list has been added at the beginning of each story to make reading easier. Each word defined on that list is printed in dark type within the story. If you forget the meaning of a word while you're reading, just check the list to review the definition.

You'll also see footnotes at the bottom of some story

pages. These notes identify people or places, explain ideas, show pronunciations, or even let you in on a joke.

We offer two other features you may wish to use. One is a two-part map of ancient Greece at the front of the book. The other is a list of the major gods, giving both their Greek and Roman names. You see, the Romans linked stories about their own gods to the Greek gods. So in many ways, the gods were identical. The list will help you keep all the names straight.

Finally at the end of each tale you'll find some more information. These revealing and sometimes amusing facts will give you insight into ancient cultures, tellers of the myths, or related myths.

One last word. Since these myths have been retold so often, many versions exist. So a story you read here may differ from a version you read elsewhere.

Now on to the myths. Remember, when you read the Retold Tales, you bring each story back to life in today's world. We hope you'll discover why these tales have earned the right to be called classics.

MAPS OF ANCIENT GREECE

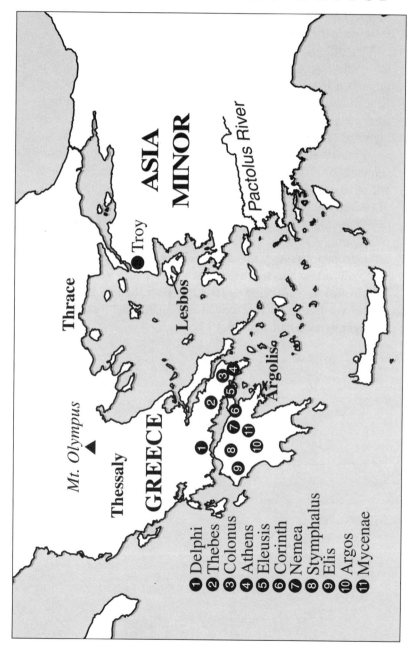

THRACE

ASIA MINOR

Pactolus River

Mt. Olympus

Thessaly

GREECE

Troy

Lesbos

Argolis

1 Delphi
2 Thebes
3 Colonus
4 Athens
5 Eleusis
6 Corinth
7 Nemea
8 Stymphalus
9 Elis
10 Argos
11 Mycenae

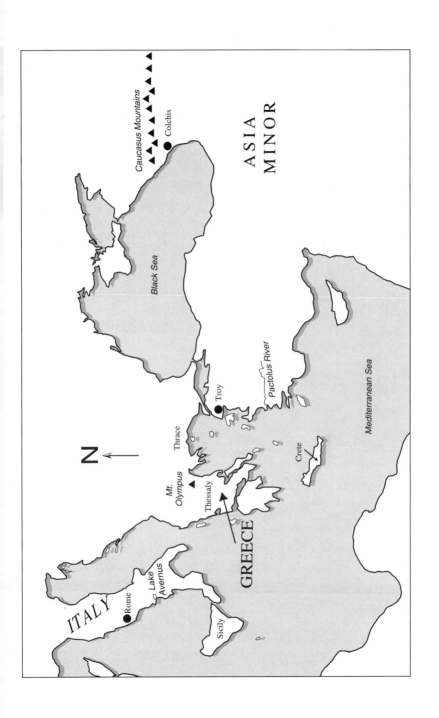

PANDORA

VOCABULARY PREVIEW

Below is a list of words that appear in the story. Read the list and get to know the words before you start the story.

abide (by)—keep faithful to; stand by
(on) behalf (of)—interest; support
caressed—touched or brushed gently
civilization—human society; culture
concede—agree; admit
destined—determined beforehand
excruciating—unbearable
famine—widespread lack of food; starvation
gloating—taking great pleasure
immortal—deathless; undying
inflict—put upon; force upon
insidious—sneaky yet harmful; underhanded
lofty—on high; heavenly
lulled—calmed; soothed
mortal—human
persuasive—convincing
plague—torment; torture
proclaimed—announced; made known
sacrifices—offerings; gifts
surge—sudden rush

PANDORA

It's a human trait to love receiving gifts. Yet as Pandora discovers, some gifts that seem to be free come with a high price tag.

High in the heavens, a horrible war raged.

On one side of this battle were the Titans.[1] These **immortal** beings had ruled earth and sky since the beginning of time. However, one day a new group of immortals—the gods—decided to overthrow the Titans.

It was a long and ugly war. But led by their king, Zeus,[2] the gods eventually defeated the Titans.

Gloating over his victory, Zeus ordered a palace to be built on Mount Olympus.[3] From there, he and the other gods controlled the heavens and the earth.

For a time it seemed as though life would remain

[1] (tī´ tanz)
[2] (zūs)
[3] (ō lim´ pus)

peaceful. Even on earth, **mortal** men lived in peace and harmony. There were no swords, spears, and helmets. There was no need for such tools of war since not a single battle had ever been fought. Neither was there any need for laws or prisons.

Not that life was perfect. Women didn't exist yet, so there were no families. And sometimes it was a struggle finding food or staying warm. But the men didn't know any other kind of life. Basically, they were happy.

Watching over the earth from his **lofty** throne, Zeus sat deep in thought. "It isn't right that these humans should just ignore the gods," Zeus said to himself. "They need to know that we control them. Otherwise, they'll become too sure of themselves. They might even try to seize power from us!"

Zeus made a decision. Bending towards the earth, he raised his thunderous voice. "From now on, men shall worship the gods," he **proclaimed.**

Hearing Zeus' booming voice, all mortals looked up to the sky in wonder.

"To show your respect, you men must kill animals and leave them to the gods as **sacrifices,**" ordered Zeus.

The men still stared upward, unsure of what to do. Then a man wrapped from head to toe in tattered cloth dared to speak. "Is it not fair that men keep part of the sacrificed animal?" he asked.

Zeus peered down at the strange-looking man. Somehow he seemed familiar. "Yes, I will **concede** to that," replied Zeus.

So the man fetched an ox and sacrificed the animal. When he stepped away from the ox, Zeus saw two piles: the skin in one portion, the bones in the other.

"You can choose which portion the gods should receive," said the man. "But will you promise to **abide** by your decision?"

"Yes," replied Zeus, "I give my word."

After all, the choice seemed an easy one to Zeus. The bones were covered with fat and must hide plenty of meat beneath.

Zeus reached down with his mighty hand and pointed to

the skin. "Men shall keep that part of the animal," he said. Reaching down with his other hand, the great god picked up the skeleton. "This part," he said, "will be kept by the gods."

The fat-covered bones fell apart in Zeus' hand. Inside were only the entrails.[4] Smiling, the strange man unfolded the skin of the ox. The cleverly hidden meat was revealed.

"On behalf of all men," said the strange man, "I thank you, great Zeus. Men shall offer the fat, bone, and entrails in sacrifice to the gods. But they shall keep the meat and skin for their own use."

Zeus realized he had been tricked. Filled with rage, he thundered, "You dare play games with me? Who do you think you are?"

The man threw off his tattered cloth, and Zeus suddenly realized why he'd looked familiar. It wasn't a man at all. Instead, the being standing before Zeus was a Titan.

"Surely you recognize me, Zeus," the Titan replied.

"Prometheus!"[5] Zeus hissed. "In the past your cleverness has proved useful to me. But don't think I'll excuse such trickery on your part. Not even on **behalf** of your precious men."

"I created men and I shall always protect them," Prometheus replied. "I'll never stop trying to help them in any way I can!"

With that, Zeus' rage boiled over. The angry thunder god raised his hand and summoned a violent storm.

Prometheus didn't stay to argue with Zeus any longer. He dashed away, taking shelter in a cave with some of the men.

As Prometheus waited out the storm, he noticed the men were shivering with cold. Also, he saw that the light was fading and it would soon be dark. Then the men wouldn't be able to see anything until morning.

Looking at the shivering, frightened mortals, Prometheus got an idea.

---

[4] Entrails are body parts such as the intestines.

[5] (prō mē´ thē us *or* prō mē´ thūs) Most Titans were imprisoned after being defeated by Zeus. Prometheus—although a Titan—was allowed to remain free because he aided Zeus in the war.

"These men need fire," he thought. "It could bring them so much—warmth, light, and heat to cook their food."

The more Prometheus thought about it, the more he realized what fire could do for humankind. Yet the Titan also knew what stood in his way.

"Zeus will never agree to let men have fire. He feels they already have too much. And if I dare bring fire down to earth anyway, Zeus will never forgive me."

But Prometheus knew what he had to do. He couldn't leave his humans in the dark and cold—no matter what punishment Zeus had in store.

So that very night, Prometheus crept to Zeus' palace on Mount Olympus. All around the palace, torches burned brightly. Yet not a soul walked the great halls.

As quietly as possible, Prometheus took a hollow reed[6] and lit it with the flame from one of the torches. Then he turned to go.

But before the Titan could reach the door, a powerful voice yelled, "Prometheus!"

Turning around, Prometheus saw Zeus approaching. "Get out of here, you wretched Titan!" yelled the king of the gods. Taking no notice of the reed Prometheus was carrying, Zeus began to hurl lightning bolts.

Prometheus wasted no time in dashing down the side of Mount Olympus. He held the reed close as he ran. He was determined that his mission be a success.

Safely back on earth, Prometheus presented his gift to men. They watched in amazement as Prometheus showed them how to use fire for light and heat and cooking. And from now on, the bones, fat, and entrails they sacrificed to the gods could be burned on their altars.

This wondrous gift of fire was the turning point for humankind. It enabled them to make great progress and start on the road to **civilization.**

That progress didn't go unnoticed. Zeus soon realized what Prometheus had done. This time, his rage was ten times

---

[6] A reed is a tall, hollow stalk of grass.

greater than before. Zeus was determined: Prometheus would never trick him again.

He had Prometheus brought before him. For a moment Zeus simply glared at the Titan. Then he said to his prisoner, "Prometheus, it was by my goodwill that you were not imprisoned with the rest of your race. But instead of appreciation, you show disobedience. I won't let you get away with this."

Prometheus looked straight at Zeus. "I did what I had to, Zeus. And now I suppose you must do what you have to."

Prometheus' words did nothing to calm Zeus. He ordered Prometheus to be chained to a rock on Mount Caucasus.[7] There the Titan suffered a terrible punishment. Every day, an eagle tore out Prometheus' liver. Then every night, Prometheus grew a new liver—which was torn out again the next day. The pain was **excruciating.**

With Prometheus out of the way, Zeus turned his thoughts to punishing mortals. In his anger, Zeus didn't care that men had really done nothing wrong.

The plan Zeus thought out was **insidious** and clever. With the help of the other gods, he created the first woman.

It was Hephaestus[8] who fashioned the woman's body from earth and water. Aphrodite[9] gave the woman beauty, and Athena[10] dressed her in fine clothes. The king of the gods added the finishing touch. He gave the woman an overpowering sense of curiosity.

Finally the woman was ready to be sent to earth. But before she left, Zeus had one last "gift" to give her.

Zeus held out a beautiful box to the woman. "This is my present to you," he told her. "But I must caution you. This box is only for looking at. You are never—under any circumstance—to open it. Remember my words. My warning is for your own good."

Zeus continued. "And now for your name. I've decided

[7] (ko´ ka sus)
[8] (he fes´ tus) Hephaestus was the god of fire and metalworking.
[9] (af ro dī´ tē) Aphrodite was the goddess of love and beauty.
[10] (a thē´ na) Athena was the goddess of wisdom and warfare.

you shall be called Pandora."[11]

Zeus had chosen a suitable name. Pandora meant "all-gifts."

Chuckling to himself in delight, Zeus called on Hermes,[12] the messenger god. "Take Pandora to Epimetheus,"[13] commanded Zeus. "Tell him this woman is a gift from all the gods."

Hermes took Pandora and the box and left. In an instant, the two completed the journey to the house of Epimetheus.

Like his brother Prometheus, Epimetheus was a Titan. Now seeing two strangers appear out of empty air, Epimetheus feared that the gods were attacking. Without stopping to take a second look, he ran inside and locked his door.

"The war is over!" shouted Epimetheus. "There's no need for the gods to **inflict** more pain upon me! Go away and leave me alone."

"Pain?" Hermes protested. "You're mistaken, Titan. I bring a gift from Zeus that would please even a god."

"If it comes from Zeus, I can guess what kind of present it is," said Epimetheus. "Take it back. After what happened to my brother, do you think I'd trust Zeus?"

In the past Prometheus had warned Epimetheus never to accept anything from Zeus. But Zeus had chosen his messenger well. Hermes was very **persuasive.**

"Why would Zeus wish you any harm?" Hermes argued. "At least take a look at his present and decide for yourself."

Cautiously, Epimetheus opened the door. When he saw Pandora, he couldn't help gasping. Her beauty was breathtaking.

"This is a woman, mortal like men," said Hermes. "But she was made in the likeness of the goddesses." Gently Hermes pushed Pandora forward.

The lovely woman walked straight to Epimetheus and took his hands in hers. "I am Pandora. I am to be your wife," she announced. Then she kissed the Titan.

---

[11](pan dō´ ra)
[12](hur´ mēz) Hermes was the messenger god, known for his swiftness.
[13](ep i mē´ thūs or ep i mē´ thē us)

"Well, if you must be my wife," Epimetheus murmured between kisses, "then my wife you shall be." He'd completely forgotten Prometheus' warning.

With a bow, Hermes left the box Zeus had sent with Pandora and vanished. But Epimetheus hardly noticed the god was gone. He simply stared at his new wife and smiled.

At last he said, "Come and see your new home." Picking up the box, he led Pandora inside the house.

"Like my brother, I do what I can to help mortal men," explained Epimetheus. "And like him, I live as simply as mortal men."

Looking around the house, Pandora said, "It doesn't matter where or how we live. Being with you is enough."

Epimetheus could hardly believe his luck. This beautiful woman seemed to be truly devoted to him.

Clearly love had clouded Epimetheus' mind. Deep down, the Titan felt there had to be a trick involved. He knew that Zeus couldn't be trusted. But Pandora's tenderness quickly **lulled** his suspicions.

Several happy weeks passed. Then one day Pandora remembered the box Zeus had given her. Slowly she walked over to the shelf where Epimetheus had placed it for safekeeping. The Titan had never touched the box again because Pandora had told him it was forbidden to open it.

Now Pandora reached out for the box and took it from the shelf.

Then Zeus' words came back to her. "You are never—under any circumstance—to open it," the great god had said. Remembering those words, Pandora quickly placed the box on the shelf once more.

But Zeus' magic began to work. Pandora burned with a powerful curiosity. Several times a day she took the box from the shelf and held it. Each time her hands **caressed** the lid, itching to open it. But each time fear overcame her curiosity.

Day after day Pandora's head was filled with only one question—what was in the box? Night after night, Pandora tossed and turned as thoughts of that box kept her from sleeping.

Epimetheus was unaware that the box haunted Pandora. All he knew was that he was happier than he'd ever been. And Pandora seemed happy too, if a little moody at times. When the Titan gazed adoringly at his wife, he had no idea she was about to change the course of the world.

One day when Epimetheus was away, Pandora took the box down from the shelf once more. She looked at it, as if trying to burn a hole through it with her gaze. She touched the lid, and her breathing quickened. Slowly, gently, she tugged at the lid.

For a brief moment, Pandora felt a **surge** of fear. She thought of Zeus' warning. Then her curiosity flooded back.

"I can't stand this anymore," she said to herself. "What harm could it do to take a quick peek inside?"

Pandora cracked the box open. Nothing. It was too dark to see inside.

Cautiously she inched the lid up another fraction. But it was still too dark.

Had Zeus been playing a trick on her? Was there anything in the box after all?

Pandora grew bolder. This time she opened the lid of the box all the way.

At once countless evils swarmed out of the box. Pandora screamed as the creatures circled her head. They were so ugly that she couldn't even look at them. Every horror of life— disease, **famine,** envy, old age, hatred, madness—filled the small house.

In a moment, the creatures found the door. As fast as Hermes himself they spread throughout the earth. And they were intent on just one thing—to **plague** mortals and make humankind miserable until the end of time.

"What have I done? What have I done?" Pandora repeated over and over. Sobbing, she slammed the lid shut and threw herself upon the box.

Pandora didn't realize that she had closed the lid just in time. In doing so, she saved the earth from complete destruction.

When he returned, Epimetheus found the weeping

Pandora still lying across the top of the box. He knew instantly what happened.

Pandora gazed at her husband with tear-filled eyes. "Can you ever forgive me?" she begged. "Can anyone ever forgive me?"

Epimetheus was full of sadness. And he felt guilty for not listening to Prometheus' warning.

But the time for guilt and blame was past. The Titan took Pandora into his arms. With gentle understanding, he forgave her.

Life on earth was now filled with grief. Yet while problems seemed to increase by the day, humans struggled on.

Other changes occurred too. As the years passed, Pandora gave birth to many daughters. Eventually the world became filled with women.

Living together side by side, men and women were **destined** to bring each other not only happiness but problems. In fact, some men claim that women caused all the miseries of the world.

But even most of those men agree that women also give men Hope. That was Pandora's gift to humankind, for Hope was the one spirit she managed to keep shut in the box. And with Hope, humans can overcome most of the evils in the world.

INSIGHTS

Prometheus—whose name means "forethought"—knew beforehand how he would be punished for giving humans fire. However, he also knew that one day he would be rescued. And in a neat twist of fate, his rescuer would prove to be Zeus' own son: Heracles.

Despite the fact that Prometheus knew his punishment wouldn't last forever, it must have seemed endless. Myths differ on how long the Titan was held captive. Some say 30 years, while others claim it was 30,000.

We tend to have special feelings for our own possessions. Prometheus was no different. He loved people so much because he had created them himself. Using a mixture of earth and water, he molded their shapes in the image of the gods. After putting the breath of life into them, he set them free on earth.

However, a first effort doesn't always prove perfect. That's why Prometheus was forever looking for ways to improve on his creation.

According to some myths, Zeus first offered Pandora to Prometheus. But Prometheus was aware of the trap Zeus had set and turned down the gift.

Zeus then gave Pandora to Epimetheus. Zeus knew that Epimetheus—whose name means "afterthought"—wouldn't discover the trick until too late.

Zeus was not all-powerful or even all-knowing. In fact, Zeus was concerned that one day someone more powerful might appear and take his place.

This is one reason Zeus created Pandora. He didn't simply want to punish humans—he also wanted to make them weaker. The supreme god feared that one day humans would rise up and try to defeat the gods.

In this myth we see Zeus as a hotheaded, selfish, vengeful god. The fact that Zeus was at first the god of thunder may account for his fearsome qualities.

Over time the Greeks came to have a different picture of Zeus. They began to view him as a noble ruler who stopped losing his temper so often. The supreme god started making his judgments based on fairness rather than emotions.

The Greeks held many festivals to honor their gods and goddesses. At the center of these celebrations were the sacrifices. At first animals were sacrificed on an altar in the open air. The sex, color, and type of animal was different for each type of god.

Animals weren't the only things sacrificed. People were free to offer anything of value—furniture, pottery, weapons, etc.

Over time temples were built, and most sacrifices were moved inside. Many of these temples were beautiful works of art. They also contained beautiful works of art: statues of the gods. The Greeks treated these statues as if they really were the gods. They washed and dressed the statues—even talked to them.

In this myth, Hope was the only creature left in the box when Pandora finally shut it. However, not all stories give the same ending.

One version tells how Pandora heard a fluttering inside the box after shutting it. This time her curiosity proved for the better. For when she opened the box, Hope flew out. By letting Hope loose, Pandora allowed this trait to spread throughout the world.

continued

Yet another version says that it wasn't Hope that was trapped in the box, but Foreknowledge. (This is the ability to tell the future.) The tellers of this myth argued that Hope is only possible if the future remains unknown.

HERACLES AND ADMETUS

VOCABULARY PREVIEW

Below is a list of words that appear in the story. Read the list
and get to know the words before you start the story.

atone—make up for
befallen—happened to
boisterous—rough and rowdy
brimming—overflowing; bursting
commotion—disturbance; uproar; racket
daunted—discouraged; disappointed
destiny—fate; future
disgraced—shamed; dishonored
distraught—troubled; upset
eerie—unearthly; ghostly
imposing—taking advantage of someone or something
jarring—harsh; unpleasant
mourning—grieving
persistent—determined; holding firm; stubborn
relish—enjoy; take pleasure in
stalked—walked stiffly and proudly
subjects—persons ruled by a king or queen
timid—lacking courage; fearful; shy
trespasser—unwelcome guest; intruder
vibrant—lively; full of energy

HERACLES
AND
ADMETUS

What would you do if you received an unwelcome guest? If the guest were a relative or friend, you'd probably know how to handle the situation. But what if the guest turned out to be a god—or even Death himself?

I've come to Thessaly[1] to be your servant for one year. Please tell me how I can help you."

King Admetus[2] could hardly believe his ears. Why would the god Apollo[3] offer to serve a mere mortal? All the king could manage to say was, "There must be some mistake. I should be *your* servant."

But there wasn't a mistake. Apollo began to tell Admetus

---

[1] (thes´ a li)
[2] (ad mē´ tus)
[3] (a pol´ ō) Apollo was the god of light and truth.

of the sad events that led to the strange request.

Apollo's son, Aesculapius,[4] had been a marvelous healer. The boy's powers were so great that he could even bring the dead back to life.

Now this alarmed Hades,[5] the god who ruled the land of the dead. If no one ever died, Hades would have no **subjects** to rule. So Hades took his worries to Zeus.[6] He begged his brother to have Aesculapius killed.

Zeus agreed that Aesculapius had too much power and planned how the boy should die. The great god ordered his workers, the Cyclopes,[7] to fashion a large bolt of lightning. Then Zeus hurled the deadly bolt at Aesculapius, killing him instantly.

When Apollo learned that his son was dead, he went crazy with anger. In his fury, he attacked the Cyclopes and killed them all.

In turn, Zeus was enraged when he learned that the Cyclopes had been killed. After all, they were innocent of wrongdoing since they'd only been obeying Zeus' orders.

As punishment, Zeus ordered Apollo to become the servant of a human for one year. "Which human do you wish to serve?" demanded Zeus.

Now Apollo didn't **relish** the thought of taking orders from a mortal. But he had no choice. After thinking for a moment, Apollo replied, "I choose Admetus, the king of Thessaly."

So here he was, standing at the king's door. Apollo again said to Admetus, "I'm at your service. I'll do whatever you ask of me."

Even after hearing Apollo's story, Admetus couldn't imagine a god being his servant. So he politely said, "Well, great Apollo, come in and have dinner with me."

---

[4] (es kū lā´ pi us)
[5] (hā´ dēz)
[6] (zūs) Zeus was the most powerful of the gods.
[7] (sī klō´ pēz) The Cyclopes were one-eyed monsters. Some say they were the sons of the sea god Poseidon.

"I come not as a guest but as a servant," Apollo replied. "Please tell me what my duties will be."

Admetus still felt uneasy giving orders to a god. But he finally said hesitantly, "I could use a herdsman right now. But I don't suppose you have any experience taking care of cattle."

Quickly Apollo answered, "In fact, I have my own herd. I shall be happy to see after yours."

So Apollo began his task of caring for King Admetus' cattle. But though Apollo insisted he was Admetus' servant, Admetus always treated him with great respect. In fact, as the months passed, the god and the king became close friends.

It was during this time that Admetus fell in love with Alcestis,[8] the daughter of Pelias.[9] Many times, Admetus had tried to visit the beautiful young Alcestis. But her father was very strict and wouldn't let any men call on his daughter. He wanted to pick her husband himself when the time came.

So Admetus could only talk to Alcestis as she sat in her window. In time, Alcestis grew to love the **persistent** king as much as he loved her.

Fearing his daughter might want to marry Admetus, Pelias told her she could marry only on one condition.

"The man you marry must take you away in a chariot pulled by lions and wild boars," Pelias said. He was sure that such a thing was impossible. Therefore, he wouldn't lose his daughter.

Now it had become customary for Admetus to visit Apollo each morning as the god herded the cattle. During one of these visits, the king told his friend and servant of Pelias' silly demand. Admetus had no idea how he was going to get wild animals to pull a chariot.

Later that day, Admetus heard a loud **commotion** in front of the palace. Running outside, he saw two lions and two boars hitched to his own chariot. The beasts, rather than being wild and dangerous, waited as patiently as **timid** sheep.

---

[8](al ses´ tis)
[9](pē´ li as)

Standing beside the chariot was Apollo. The god smiled and bowed to Admetus when he saw the king's astonished gaze.

"How lucky I am to have a god on my side!" exclaimed the king.

"Think nothing of it," said Apollo. "Now you can bring your lady home in style."

Immediately Admetus jumped into the chariot and rode it straight to Pelias' home. Alcestis nearly fell out her window when she saw the lions and boars pulling Admetus' chariot. Admetus simply smiled at her and waved.

Pelias, too, was astonished when he saw the chariot. "Only a man blessed by the gods could have accomplished this," he thought. This made it a little easier for him to give up his daughter and agree to the marriage.

In the months following their wedding, the young couple grew to love each other even more deeply. Apollo delighted in watching the happy king and queen.

Finally Apollo's year of service came to an end. Apollo prepared to return home with some regret. He would miss his mortal friends.

When the time came to leave, Apollo went to the palace to bid the king and queen good-bye.

Apollo was shocked at what he found. Lying in bed, the usually **vibrant** king was deathly ill. His handsome face was pale and thin, and his once bright eyes were dark and sunken.

Frightened by her husband's condition, Alcestis pleaded to Apollo for advice. "What should I do?" she asked. "I fear he's dying."

In a weak voice, Admetus said, "Apollo, my friend, what cruel luck has **befallen** me! Finally I'm married to the woman I love. And what happens? Death has come to take me before I'm ready."

Apollo looked at the king with deep concern. "I'll try to help you, my friend," he said. With that, the god disappeared in a flash of light.

Apollo went to find the Fates. These three goddesses knew how long a person would live. When Apollo found them, he fearfully asked them when Admetus would die.

One of the Fates held up the thread that measured the length of Admetus' life. "This shows that Admetus is going to die very soon," she explained.

"Can't you make the thread longer?" asked Apollo.

The three Fates refused. "We never change a person's fate," one said stubbornly.

Apollo wasn't **daunted** by their answer. Instead, he smiled and began to argue. Apollo never raised his voice or showed anger. He simply talked on and on in a gentle, reasonable way.

After quite some time, the Fates ran out of reasons why Admetus should die.

"Stop!" one of the goddesses cried. "We'll agree to your request on one condition. Admetus can live—but only if he finds someone to die in his place."

Apollo returned to Admetus' bedside to deliver the news. Then wishing the king good luck, the god vanished.

By this time Admetus had grown very weak and couldn't even leave his bed. So the king's servants brought many people to him who might die in his place. And to each visitor, Admetus asked the same question: "Will you die in my place?"

First came the brave warriors of Admetus' army. The king had led them in many victories. Before each battle, they'd claimed they would gladly give their lives for the king. But now, looking upon the pale and dying Admetus, the warriors forgot their promises. None would trade places with their leader.

Next came Admetus' loyal servants. They'd all enjoyed good lives under the protection of the royal family. Again, none could bear the thought of giving their lives for Admetus. Even the old ones who would die soon anyway refused.

At last Admetus called for his own parents. Surely they would be willing to save their son. But like all the others, neither his mother nor father would meet Death in Admetus' place.

Alone at last with Alcestis, Admetus moaned in

desperation. "That's it, then," he gasped. "I am lost. No one will give up life for me."

Alcestis looked at her husband. "I will," she replied in a steady voice.

Admetus smiled at her and squeezed her hand. He shook his head to refuse her offer. But before he could say no, the exchange took place.

Immediately Admetus regained his color and energy. Just as quickly, Alcestis grew pale and fell to the floor.

Jumping out of bed, Admetus picked up his devoted wife. Gently he placed her on the bed. "No!" he cried. "Alcestis, don't leave me!"

But it was no use. Within moments, the beautiful queen was dead.

Overcome by grief, Admetus dropped to the floor and wept. For a long time he held his wife's cold hands.

At last when morning dawned, the king rose. He told himself he must put his grief aside and do his duty. He had plans to make—plans for an elaborate funeral to honor his beloved wife.

The day of the funeral arrived and a hush fell over the kingdom. Admetus' servants went quietly about their tasks.

But into that quiet came a **jarring** noise. A thundering knock was heard at the palace doors. Then a giant bull of a man wearing a lion's skin as armor and a lion's head as a helmet marched into the palace. In a booming voice, he yelled, "Admetus! Where are you?"

The servants immediately scattered to all corners. They feared a monster had come to attack the king. Some ran off to warn him about the fearsome attacker.

However, Admetus needed no warning. He'd heard the stranger's rumbling voice and now rushed into the main hall. But before the king could say a word, the huge visitor cried out, "Admetus!" Then he lunged forward and gripped the king tightly.

The alarmed servants started to dart to their king's rescue. But the stranger caught sight of their worried faces. With a booming laugh, he released Admetus and asked, "What? Have the years so changed me that no one here recognizes Heracles?"[10]

Admetus gave a sad smile. "As you say, my friend, it has been many years since you've paid me a visit. But while your face may not be as familiar here as I would like, your name and deeds are known to all."

Indeed, Heracles was one of the greatest heroes of that age—or any other. Tales of his strength and daring were treasured gold.

In fact, Heracles had just come from an adventure. Now he wanted to relax at his friend's home before charging ahead to his next challenge. Heracles looked forward to talking, laughing, and feasting with the king. The two had spent many such evenings together.

A thoughtful look came over the hero's face. "Admetus, it's good to see you again. But something in your face speaks of sadness. Have I come at a bad time?" he asked.

Admetus couldn't tell Heracles the truth. A good friend didn't burden others with sorrow. And a good host didn't make a guest feel like he was **imposing.**

So Admetus answered, "A servant of mine died. His funeral is today. But I insist that you stay here. You know you're always welcome."

Admetus ordered his servants to show Heracles to a guest room. Then the king called all his servants together.

"I want you to take special care of my friend," he ordered. "That includes not telling him the truth about who has died. If he found out, he'd refuse to stay here."

So while Alcestis' funeral took place, Heracles merrily feasted. Hungry as a bear at the end of winter, he ordered dish after dish from the servants. And he kept the wine streaming like a waterfall into his cup.

Not surprisingly, Heracles became quite drunk. He danced around the room and sang loud, **boisterous** songs. These songs were the type that sailors and soldiers sang—hardly proper for a house in **mourning.**

---

[10](her´ a klēz) He was also known as *Hercules* (her´ kū lēz).

All day the servants came in pairs to serve Heracles—they were afraid to face the giant man alone. And in their faces, Heracles saw growing disapproval. Finally Heracles could stand their dark mood no longer.

"Why don't you smile?" he yelled at the next servants to bring him refreshments. "Have some wine! Sing with me!"

"It wouldn't be right, sir," the nervous servants replied.

"By my father Zeus, you'll drink with me right now!" yelled Heracles. He dragged both servants to the table and poured them some wine. But the servants again refused to drink.

"What's the matter with you?" Heracles demanded. "Was this servant who died so special?"

One servant nodded. The other whispered, "Very special."

Looking into their eyes, Heracles began to have doubts. He grabbed one of them in each hand and lifted them off the floor.

"Tell me what's going on around here," said Heracles, "and tell me fast."

Fearfully, one of the servants replied, "Today our queen, Alcestis, was buried."

Heracles dropped the servants to the floor.

"I should have known," he said. "Admetus' eyes were dark as the pits of Hades. He looked as if he'd been chasing sleep for days."

Slamming his huge fists onto the table, Heracles cursed himself. "While my friend buries his wife," he cried, "I've carried on like a fool! I've wronged him!"

Heracles paced the floor, wondering how he could make things right. Suddenly an idea struck him. Heracles immediately went in search of Admetus.

He found his host sitting alone on a bench. Tears streamed down the king's weary, pale face.

Dropping to his knees, Heracles grasped Admetus' hands in his own.

"I'm so sorry, my friend," said Heracles. "I must **atone** for my drunken behavior in your time of grief. You kept the truth from me just to be a good host. And I **disgraced** myself."

Admetus tried to say something to calm the **distraught** Heracles. However, before the king could reply, Heracles stood up.

"But I have a plan, my friend. I know what I'll do to make up for my rudeness."

Before Admetus could speak a word, Heracles strode out of the room. Admetus stared after him in wonder.

Some say Heracles wasn't a great thinker. And if Admetus had known his friend's plan...Well, even he might have wondered about Heracles' wisdom.

But the great hero would have just laughed at his doubters. To Heracles, a person who thought too long just became tied up in fears. He knew his strength. And he knew that it was his **destiny** to attempt deeds others didn't even dream of.

So without a second thought, Heracles put on his lion's skin armor and lion's head helmet and headed straight for a place few living humans had ever been: the underworld.

At the gates of the underworld, Heracles met Cerberus.[11] This vicious three-headed dog stood guard over the kingdom of the dead. Should any living creatures approach, Cerberus would tear them into scraps.

Now Cerberus leaped at Heracles, all three heads of teeth snapping. But with one powerful blow, Heracles sent the dog spinning against the gates of the underworld. Then stepping over the stunned animal, he marched into the land of the dead.

The world Heracles entered was a chilly, gloomy place, filled with gray mist. **Eerie** sounds echoed through the land. The forms of dead people drifted about. Yet Heracles strode onwards, as though the sights and sounds were as ordinary as those in the marketplace.

Suddenly Hades—the fearsome god of the underworld—stood before Heracles.

"What are you doing here?" the god coldly demanded. "You know no living mortals are permitted in this place."

[11](ser´ ber us)

"Then leave me to my business, Lord Hades, and I'll be away. Just show me Death."

"I can show you death in many forms, Heracles," the god threatened.

Heracles raised his eyebrows. Then he laughed. "No doubt, great god. But I'm not interested in anything for myself today. Now where is old man Death?"

Just then Heracles caught sight of what he'd been looking for. In the distance, Death **stalked** among the shadows. And across his shoulder, Death carried a lovely burden: the body of Alcestis.

"If you will excuse me, Lord Hades," Heracles said. He brushed past the god.

Hades watched him go but made no move to stop him. "I do not willingly excuse you, Heracles," he murmured. "But your father would doubtless teach me my manners if I forgot how to treat a guest."

In the meantime, Heracles caught up with Death. "Old man!" he shouted. "Wait up. There's no need to rush off like that. In fact, I think you've been hasty in this case. Perhaps even a little greedy."

Death simply stared at the hero, unable to believe the nerve of this **trespasser.** "Leave, mortal. Be glad that I'm not greedy enough to claim your body today."

Heracles still stood firmly in Death's path. "I've come for the queen," he calmly announced. Then in a second, he'd snatched Alcestis' body from Death and gently laid her on the ground.

The hero turned back to Death with a grin. "If you want the queen, old man, you'll have to outwrestle me first."

"Do you dare deny destiny? This woman was fated to die."

"And do you think I could have reached the underworld if the gods had not allowed it?" Heracles replied. "I'm fated to rescue her."

Death again stared at Heracles. This time he said not a word but just reached out to reclaim Alcestis' body.

Heracles quickly grabbed Death by the shoulder. With

that, the wrestling match began.

Now everyone knows that Death has a powerful hold. Once Death gets a grip on someone, he rarely lets go. But Heracles was a man **brimming** with life. He'd already escaped Death several times.

So the match was fairly even for a while. Sometimes one would try a tricky hold or make a quick throw. But for a long time, neither Death nor Heracles could gain the upper hand.

Finally, though, Heracles' living strength made the difference. He grasped Death by the neck and fixed a powerful hold. Tighter and tighter he squeezed.

At last Death gasped, "Enough! Take the woman."

Heracles stepped back. "You are most merciful, Death," he said with a grin. Then he lightly scooped up the queen into his arms.

"She'll be mine in time anyway, mortal," Death growled. "As will you."

"That's not up to me or you but the gods," Heracles replied. "But should we be destined to meet again, I trust you'll remember I don't like being rushed. Especially by Death."

As Heracles walked back through the gates of the underworld, Hades did nothing to stop him. Even Cerberus watched calmly as Heracles passed.

Back in Thessaly, Admetus still sat motionless in his chair. His tears had dried. Yet the pain and darkness in his eyes had only deepened. His beloved wife was dead—dead because he had so selfishly tried to cling to life.

Admetus never even noticed the shouts outside the palace or the sound of running feet. But he did hear the scream of a servant who waited beside his chair.

Looking up, the king saw a vision from his dreams. There stood Alcestis—alive, healthy, and beautiful.

Admetus gasped and rose from his chair. Then he and his wife rushed into each other's arms. Their embrace of love was more fierce than any Heracles and Death had used.

"How…?" whispered Admetus.

Alcestis turned. There stood the obvious answer: Heracles.

"Heracles," Admetus gasped. "You've done the impossible. You've—"

"Only tried to make up for my rude behavior," Heracles said. "Stay well, my friends." Then as abruptly as he'd arrived, the hero left.

Still in shock, Admetus said softly, "Come back anytime, my friend. My wife and I will be in debt to you to our dying days."

Then staring in wonder at Alcestis, he added, "And beyond."

INSIGHTS

The god Apollo was grateful for Admetus' respectful treatment. To show his appreciation, Apollo threw in some work only a god could do. He caused all Admetus' cows to bear twins, thereby enlarging Admetus' herd.

Heracles' superhuman strength is not surprising, considering he was part god. He was the son of the god Zeus and a mortal woman named Alcmene.

Heracles first demonstrated his strength when he was just a baby. One night he and his brother were asleep when two huge snakes crawled into their bedroom and tried to attack them. Heracles' brother screamed in terror. But brave Heracles caught the snakes in his hands and strangled them.

The giant snakes were only the first of many challenges Heracles faced during the course of his life. As an adult, he undertook a series of twelve tasks, or *labors*. Each of these tasks called for Heracles to use his bravery and muscles.

Heracles' first labor involved killing the fierce lion of Nemea. Heracles tried to destroy the gigantic animal with his club and arrows. When this failed, he managed to kill the lion as he had the snakes—by strangling it with his bare hands.

From then on, Heracles wore the Nemean lion's skin—but not just as a trophy. The lion's head served as his helmet. And the beast's skin offered protection as tough as armor.

Death was wrong about Heracles. Though the hero died a very painful death, he didn't descend to the underworld as Death thought. Instead, Heracles was taken to live with the gods on Olympus.

continued

According to one myth, Heracles wasn't responsible for Alcestis' rescue from the underworld at all. In this story, Persephone—the queen of the underworld—thought it evil that a wife should die in place of her husband. So she sent Alcestis back to earth to finish out her life.

Even if he really didn't rescue Alcestis, Heracles was no stranger to Hades. During one of his adventures, he was asked to bring the watchdog Cerberus back to earth.

Heracles also rescued Theseus, another hero, from the underworld. Theseus foolishly tried to kidnap Persephone, the beautiful wife of Hades. As punishment, Hades—the god of the underworld—had glued Theseus to a chair.

Admetus had his hands full preparing Alcestis' funeral. For Greeks, funerals were quite an affair. First the dead body was bathed and covered with perfumes. Flowers were placed on the person's head. And the corpse was dressed in the finest clothes the family could afford.

On the third day after death the body was carried in a procession to the gravesite. During the procession the women wept loudly and beat their breasts. (Sometimes professional mourners were hired to do this and to sing sad songs.)

Over the covered grave wine was poured and an animal was often sacrificed as food for the departed soul. Mourners—who wore black clothes—sometimes cut off some of their hair as a gift for the dead. Then the mourners laid flowers on the grave and went back home to the funeral feast.

The grave wasn't forgotten, though. Children of the dead person visited it often and offered food and drink to their parent's soul.

According to the poet Homer, Hades was a gloomy place full of the ghosts of those who died—good as well as bad. Later poets described Hades as a place where the evil were punished and the good rewarded.

According to these later sources, the dead souls were

placed before three judges who passed sentence. The wicked were immediately sent to their everlasting punishment. The good, on the other hand, went to the Elysian Fields. There, surrounded by sunny meadows and shady woods, the fortunate Greeks lived in peace and happiness

Then there were those who never made it to Hades at all. The Greeks believed a person had to be properly buried before he or she would be allowed into the underworld. So until these poor souls received their funeral, they had to wander the banks of the river just outside Hades.

Hades was a place most Greeks preferred not to see till the proper time. However, there were others besides Heracles who risked journeying to the underworld.

Perhaps the story of Orpheus is closest to Heracles' adventure. Orpheus, a wonderful Greek musician, refused to accept the death of his beloved wife, Eurydice. So he journeyed to the underworld to try to bring her back.

But unlike Heracles, Orpheus used art instead of muscle to win his argument. The gods were so moved by his music that they allowed Eurydice to leave with her husband.

However, the story didn't end as happily as Heracles' mission. Though he was warned not to gaze at his wife until he reached the upper world, Orpheus' will failed him. He looked back at Eurydice—and lost her again.

THE JUDGMENT OF PARIS

VOCABULARY PREVIEW

Below is a list of words that appear in the story. Read the list and get to know the words before you start the story.

blissful—delightful; heavenly
coax—persuade; sway
court—try to win the affection of
discord—conflict; disagreement
frail—delicate; weak
handiwork—result of one's efforts
impartial—treating all equally; fair
irresistible—having great appeal; impossible to ignore
mutual—shared; in common
proclaimed—publicly announced; made known
prompt—remind or suggest what to say or do; push
recited—spoke; repeated
resemblance—likeness; similarity
safeguard—something that offers protection
shallow—lacking feeling; meaningless; empty
shrewd—clever; smart
tending—taking care of
treaty—agreement; pledge
unison—at the same time; harmony
wage—engage in

The
JUDGMENT
of PARIS

Young Paris is given the chance of a lifetime. To win a priceless prize, he only has to give his judgment. But Paris foolishly forgets that a judge may himself be judged—and convicted.

rom the day Paris was born, people knew he was destined to bring trouble to those who loved him.

Even his parents—King Priam and Queen Hecuba of Troy[1]—feared their new baby. Many times Hecuba dreamed that the child would cause the ruin of Troy. Clearly the gods were warning them.

Though the parents had so many doubts about their child, they didn't have the heart to kill him. Instead, they decided to send Paris away from the city.

Following the king's orders, a servant delivered Paris to a shepherd. The shepherd took the child to his home on Mount Ida and raised him.

[1] (prī´ am)(hek´ u ba)(troi)

Paris happily took to the life of a shepherd. And it seemed to suit him in more than spirit. Though somewhat **frail,** the boy grew into a remarkably handsome young man.

Secrets are rarely kept very long, and Paris' true identity was no exception. At an early age, Paris learned about his royal parents. But this knowledge didn't bother him.

"If my mother and father don't want me, then the feeling is **mutual,**" he told himself. "What do I need with a palace and servants when I have this beautiful mountainside?"

In fact, Paris fully expected to live on Mount Ida **tending** sheep until the day he died. But fate held a strange twist for the young prince. The day came when Paris became one of the most important people in world history.

Why did Paris have such an impact on destiny? Did he **wage** war or build kingdoms?

No, he served as judge in a beauty contest.

This strange thread of events began to unravel at a wedding. It was a special wedding since the great hero Peleus[2] was marrying the sea goddess Thetis.[3]

Many gods and goddesses attended the celebration. However, one goddess wasn't invited—and for good reason. No one wanted Eris,[4] the goddess of **discord,** to be present. After all, who needed arguments on such a happy occasion?

Furious and bitter, Eris came up with a clever plan to pay everyone back for being ignored. Just as all the guests were sitting down to a feast, she threw a golden apple among them.

One of the gods picked up the apple. "This is curious," he commented. "The apple says, 'For the fairest.' "

Immediately all the goddesses demanded to be awarded the apple. Finally after much argument, all but three of the goddesses gave up. These stubborn goddesses were Hera,[5] Athena,[6] and Aphrodite.[7]

The three goddesses approached Zeus,[8] king of the gods.

---

[2] (pē´ lūs *or* pē´ lē us)
[3] (thē´ tis)
[4] (ē´ ris *or* er´ is)
[5] (hē´ ra *or* her´ a)

They asked him to decide who deserved the apple.

It just so happened that Zeus was married to Hera. So naturally he was reluctant to get involved in the argument.

"I would have a hard time being **impartial**," Zeus told them. "Can't you simply share the apple?"

The three goddesses glared at him. Hera spoke for them all. "We demand a judgment," she said.

"Very well!" said Zeus. "If you must finish this foolish contest, I'll give you a judge. Go to Mount Ida and find the young shepherd Paris. Ask him to decide which one of you is most beautiful."

Nearly in **unison,** the three goddesses asked, "Why Paris?"

Zeus shrugged his shoulders. "Paris isn't just a shepherd. He's the son of King Priam of Troy. He's handsome enough to be a god himself. And he has a god's eye for beauty. But I warn you, you must accept his decision. It will be final."

The goddesses agreed to accept Paris as judge. Once the decision was made, they wasted no time. Racing through the sky, they glowed like falling stars. In a matter of moments, they'd flown to Mount Ida.

Imagine Paris' surprise when he found himself surrounded by three of the most beautiful women he'd ever seen.

"Who are you? And why have you come here?" Paris asked them in amazement.

Aphrodite explained, "I'm Aphrodite, goddess of love and beauty. This is Hera, the goddess who protects marriage. And this is Athena, goddess of wisdom. We've come to you for a judgment. You must decide which one of us is the most beautiful. Whatever your decision, Zeus will make sure that we accept it."

Paris stared at them in bewilderment. "But to judge three goddesses. Three such beautiful goddesses—"

Hera quickly moved forward. "—is an honor you cannot

[6] (a thē´ na)
[7] (af ro dī´ tē)
[8] (zūs)

refuse. Come, my young friend. Step into the light so you may judge me without any doubts."

The queen of heaven dragged Paris around a large rock to **coax** him in private.

"I know this will be a difficult decision for you, Paris," Hera said in her most honeyed voice. "But Zeus wouldn't have chosen you unless you were fair. The fact that my husband knows of your qualities must mean great things await you."

Hera lowered her voice. "In fact, I could guarantee that. If you should prove your wisdom by choosing me, I'll give you power beyond any mortal's. I'll make you ruler of all Europe and Asia."

Paris didn't have time to reply, for Athena suddenly appeared. With a firm grip, the goddess pulled him away.

"My turn, Hera," she declared. "Come, shepherd. I'll show you a beauty that lights up the darkest night." The goddess herded Paris into a nearby cave.

"Now listen, Paris," Athena began. "I know that once you make up your mind, you'll stick to your opinion. Zeus wouldn't have suggested you as judge unless you had the will of a warrior. So whatever decision you reach, I'll respect you for it."

Paris bowed his head, unable to look into the goddess' gleaming gray eyes.

"But a warrior should also know what's at stake when he enters a contest. If you choose me, I'll make you the world's most famous warrior. You'll defeat any opponent in battle. In fact, you'll lead the Trojans to victory against the Greeks."

Again Paris' reply was cut off. From outside the cave came the lovely voice he'd first heard. "Dear young shepherd, surely it's my turn to speak with you?"

Almost in a daze, Paris followed the sound of the voice. Aphrodite waited for him to reach her side. Then linking arms with him, she led Paris out into a nearby meadow.

For a time, the goddess said nothing. Then she sighed and turned to her companion.

"It pains me to say this, Paris, but I know that the others were trying to bribe you," she remarked.

Paris felt a blush rise to his cheeks as the goddess watched him with her glorious eyes.

"I can guess what they offered you, Paris: great power. But whether on the throne or battlefield, power's a **shallow** thing. It means taking and hurting. It means blinding yourself to beauty for fear that beauty might weaken you. It means being lonely and loveless because no one is your equal."

The goddess studied Paris for a moment. "And what's more important than love and beauty, dear Paris?"

Aphrodite leaned closer. "I'll tell you the answer: nothing. And I'll prove it to you. Choose me as the fairest, and I'll give you the most beautiful woman in the world."

She softly touched his cheek. "Isn't that what your heart truly desires?"

"Enough!" came a voice from behind them.

Paris turned to find Hera and Athena approaching. Hera spoke again. "Paris has had a chance to study us all. Now it's time for his decision."

In confusion, Paris looked from one goddess to another. Finally he said, "Can I think it over?"

"Very well," they agreed.

As the three of them stood in front of Paris, they tapped their feet impatiently. Barely able to concentrate under this pressure, Paris tried to think over the situation.

"I have no desire to be a ruler or a warrior," he admitted to himself. "I've always been a weakling and am really a coward at heart. But to have the most beautiful woman in the world as my own..."

For the past two years, Paris had been married to a lovely young woman named Oenone.[9] Paris was truly fond of his wife. Yet beautiful women still held a strong attraction for him. Yes, Aphrodite's offer was very appealing.

Paris finally looked up at the goddesses. Once more he weighed each. Then he announced simply, "Aphrodite is the most beautiful."

[9] (ē nō´ nē)

Athena and Hera burned with disappointment. They decided on the spot that all Trojans deserved bad fortune.

Without a word, they vanished into the sky. Paris gazed upwards with concern in his eyes. "Do you think…I hope they understand…" He came to a worried stop.

Aphrodite just laughed. "Don't worry about them. Now it's time to talk of your reward."

Paris looked at her eagerly. "The most beautiful woman in the world!" he exclaimed. "Who is she?"

"Helen of Sparta,"[10] Aphrodite replied.

Having lived his life among the shepherds, Paris knew little of the outside world. Yet even he had heard of Helen. "But isn't she married to King Menelaus?"[11] Paris protested.

"I told you not to worry, Paris. Helen will find you **irresistible.** I can guarantee that."

Aphrodite neglected to tell Paris the whole story of Helen. The beautiful young woman was the daughter of Zeus. However, Leda,[12] Helen's mother, was human. King Tyndareus[13] had married Helen's mother and raised the young Helen as his own daughter.

By the time Helen was old enough for marriage, people far and wide knew of her beauty. Many of the greatest kings, princes, and warriors of Greece came to **court** Helen.

One day, a riot nearly broke out in the main hall of the palace. All the men who wanted to marry Helen had gathered there. Claiming that Tyndareus had stalled long enough, they demanded that he choose one of them to become Helen's husband.

Tyndareus could see how angry and dangerous the men were. He realized choosing one man would turn the others against himself and the lucky husband. Tyndareus sought out Odysseus,[14] the clever king of Ithaca,[15] for a solution. Since he was already married, Odysseus wasn't competing for Helen.

---

[10](spar´ ta)
[11](men e lā´ us)
[12](lē´ da)
[13](tin dā´ rē us)

Odysseus thought over the matter and suggested making all of Helen's admirers take an oath.

"Have them swear to defend the man who marries Helen if anything ever threatens the marriage," Odysseus urged.

Tyndareus clapped Odysseus on the back gratefully. "You're a **shrewd** man, my friend," said Tyndareus.

By the time Tyndareus returned to the main hall, men were throwing tables and chairs at each other. They were even vowing to start wars. The king demanded silence. When the men calmed down enough to listen, Tyndareus explained Odysseus' plan to them.

The men really had no choice. After all, each one hoped to be the lucky husband of Helen. So they agreed to the oath.

When this was done, Tyndareus announced his decision. He chose King Menelaus of Sparta to marry Helen. Beaming with pride and happiness, Menelaus led the beautiful Helen away. The other men watched with red faces, grumbling and griping bitterly. But no one dared go back on the oath.

In this way the marriage of Helen and Menelaus carried an unusual **safeguard.** The oath served as a **treaty** among all the kingdoms of Greece.

Paris knew nothing about this oath as he happily set out for Sparta. He was confident that Aphrodite's spell would help him win Helen's heart in no time.

When he arrived at the palace in Sparta, Paris introduced himself to King Menelaus.

"I am Paris, the son of King Priam of Troy," Paris explained.

Menelaus gladly welcomed the young prince. Under Priam's leadership, Troy had become a mighty kingdom. Other kings wanted to stay on good terms with the powerful Trojan king.

Menelaus wasn't the only one who welcomed Paris. In spite of herself, Helen felt powerfully attracted to Paris. This young, godlike stranger looked far different from her husband. Stocky, bearded, and aging, Menelaus was not a very dramatic

[14](ō dis´ ūs *or* ō dis´ ē us)
[15](ith´ a ka)

figure. He'd never have been the man she'd have chosen to marry.

As for his part, Paris fell deeply in love with Helen the moment they met. He began romancing Helen almost immediately. For her pleasure, he sang songs and **recited** poetry. He showed Helen a thousand kindnesses and paid her countless compliments.

But Paris took care to hide what he was doing. Menelaus had no idea that the young prince was trying to sweep Helen away.

After a few weeks, Menelaus was called away on urgent business. He bid farewell to his wife without a single worry.

As the king departed, Paris and Helen shyly turned to one another.

"Forgive my boldness, Queen Helen," Paris begged. "But I must confess my feelings for you. I have seen many lovely women in my day, but none lovelier than you. I have known kindness before, but no generosity can match yours. I have known gentle spirits, true—but none as sweet as your own."

The young man sank to his knees. "I love you, Helen. "

Helen drew a deep, shaky breath. In that moment she weighed her duty as a wife against her desire as a young woman. Did Aphrodite **prompt** her? It must have been so, for at last Helen whispered, "And I love you."

Paris laughed for joy. Drawing Helen close, he urged, "Then you must come away with me. I can't stand seeing you live as another man's wife. When we're far from here, no one will be able to come between us."

Helen again hesitated—but not for long. Life with the man she adored sounded so much better than staying with Menelaus.

"Yes, my love," Helen decided. "I'll come with you."

By nightfall, Paris and Helen had packed Helen's belongings. She didn't take much with her. In fact, she even left her young daughter behind. Some said this proved what a selfish woman Helen was. Others said it only showed how unhappy she'd been. Still others said that it was evidence that she was under one of Aphrodite's spells.

Whatever the goddess' role, she did at least keep watch over Helen and Paris. She saw that they safely reached Mount Ida. There the lovers spent several **blissful** days.

But before long, Paris grew dissatisfied with his old home. He decided to take Helen to his parents' palace in Troy.

"I've never even seen my parents," Paris told Helen. "But I'm still their son. And I want you to live like a queen, not a shepherd's wife."

For a moment Paris guiltily thought of Oenone, the wife he'd deserted. But he quickly forgot her as he gazed into Helen's lovely eyes.

Once again, Aphrodite saw that the couple safely completed their journey. Paris confidently entered King Priam's hall, with Helen by his side.

Priam and Hecuba stared in shock at the young man. The family **resemblance** was so strong, they recognized him immediately.

"Priam," gasped Hecuba. "Is it possible?"

The king's eyes filled with tears. "My son! For so many years I've longed to see you. Surely this is a sign that all trouble has passed!"

Overcome with love, the royal couple threw their arms around Paris. In their joy, they eagerly put aside their earlier fears that their son would cause Troy's ruin. They both urged Paris to live with them in the palace.

Paris was touched by his parents' loving welcome. And once they explained the terrible signs surrounding his birth, he understood why they'd sent him away.

"It was all for the best that you did send me to live among the shepherds," Paris told his parents. "I found my destiny there."

He drew Helen forward. "Mother and Father, this is Helen, my bride-to-be," he announced proudly.

"Now you shall be Helen of Troy," **proclaimed** Priam, smiling at the young woman.

Wasting no time, Priam called for a huge wedding celebration. Aphrodite herself attended the feast, disguised as a servant. She smiled at the happy couple, satisfied with her own **handiwork.**

But of course this wedding—just like that of Peleus and Thetis—was destined to end in discord. For when Menelaus returned and found his wife and guest gone, he flew into a rage.

"Does that beardless dog think he can run off with my wife?" he roared. Immediately he sent word to all the kings, princes, and warriors who had taken the oath.

When they arrived, Menelaus announced, "The day has come to fulfill your pledge. Paris of Troy has taken my wife. I call upon you to help me bring her back to Sparta."

The Greeks kept their word and gathered their armies. And while Paris and his family dreamed of peace and happiness, the Greeks dreamed of glory and easy victory. Ten long years later, both would find out how false their dreams had been.

Now as the Greek ships set sail for Troy, Athena and Hera watched with satisfaction. "At last the wheels are in motion!" Hera exclaimed. "Now we'll have our revenge against Paris— and all the miserable Trojans."

The goddess Eris also watched and smiled. How well her plan had worked! And the fools had never guessed that her golden apple had been rotten to the core.

INSIGHTS

Eris was also known by another name, Discordia. It should be no surprise that we get our word *discord* from this name.

Discordia's brothers were probably also unwelcome at celebrations. Their names were Fear, Panic, Terror, and Trembling.

Homer, a Greek poet who is said to have told the story of the Trojan War, is a mythic figure himself. No one knows if there really was a Homer. Or if he did exist, was he really blind as legends say?

According to some tales, the story of Paris and Helen is said to explain Homer's blindness. Homer said that Helen willingly went with Paris to Troy. However, many Greeks believed Helen was kidnapped against her will. These Greeks said that Homer was struck blind for his lie.

It probably didn't surprise the Greeks that Paris chose a beautiful woman over power. The Greeks had a great love for anything beautiful—be it humans, pottery, or architecture.

The women of Sparta—where Helen was from—went so far as to place a figure of Apollo in their bedrooms. (Apollo was said to be one of the most beautiful gods.) In this way the women hoped to bear beautiful children.

Oenone—Paris' first wife—got her revenge in the end. But it proved to be bittersweet.

During the Trojan War, Paris was wounded by a Greek warrior's poisoned arrow. Oenone, who was nearby, refused to help her unfaithful husband. Paris was overcome by the poison and soon died.

continued

However, Oenone apparently still felt some love for Paris. For after he died, Oenone killed herself out of grief.

The troublesome apple in the story grew on a tree in the Garden of the Hesperides. This garden was guarded by three nymphs (minor goddesses) and a dragon.

In spite of the guards, others besides Eris were able to obtain some of the golden fruit. The great hero Heracles managed to get some golden apples. And three of the apples played a part in a fateful race between the lovers Atalanta and Hippomenes—which you can read about in this book.

Most Greeks believed that Helen was the daughter of the god Zeus and the mortal woman Leda. It was said that Zeus made love to Leda after changing himself into a swan. As a result of their union, Leda gave birth to two sets of twins at the same time.

However, only one set of twins—Helen and Pollux—were children of Zeus. The other two—Castor and Clytemnestra—were fathered by Leda's human husband, Tyndareus.

In time the Trojan War turned into a war of the gods. Aphrodite, of course, favored the Trojans. And Hera and Athena were true to their word in defending the Greeks.

Gradually all the gods on Olympus took sides. The supreme god Zeus secretly liked the Trojans best. But he tried to act neutral so he wouldn't make Hera angry.

The gods did their best to influence the action of the human warriors. They appeared to them in dreams and told them what to do. Sometimes the gods even acted like children playing with toy soldiers, snatching their favorites out of the way of enemy swords.

Despite the gods' best efforts, fate won out in the end and Troy was destroyed.

AGAMEMNON AND CLYTEMNESTRA

VOCABULARY PREVIEW

Below is a list of words that appear in the story. Read the list and get to know the words before you start the story.

appease—calm; soothe; make peace with
arms—weapons
compromising—reaching an agreement by combining two or more solutions
confirmed—proven to be true
conspiring—plotting; scheming
distract—turn aside; sidetrack; draw away
entangled—caught up in; trapped
executioner—one who carries out a death sentence
feuded—quarreled or fought, often for a long time
grisly—sickening; disgusting
haunting—eerie; disturbing; memorable
heir—person entitled to inherit something, such as property or a title
humility—humbleness; obedience
insolent—disrespectful; making fun of
malicious—wicked; full of evil
parched—dry
sacred—holy; blessed
signified—meant; made known
slew—killed; murdered
tempestuous—violent; wild; fierce

Agamemnon
and
Clytemnestra

Is there ever a good reason for murder? The unhappy family in this myth believes so. But once the killing has begun, they'll find it very hard to stop.

In the distance at the top of a tower, a fire burned brightly. Watching from the palace at Mycenae, Queen Clytemnestra[1] smiled. "So my dear husband is still alive," she thought. "It won't be long before he arrives home."

Wanting to be ready with a special welcome, Clytemnestra had arranged this signal. She had asked her husband Agamemnon[2] to light a fire on Mount Ida when the war ended. The clever queen then arranged for the signal to be relayed from tower to mountaintop until it reached Mycenae.

For ten long years, Agamemnon had been away at Troy[3]

[1] (mī sē´ nē)(klītem nes´ tra)
[2] (ag a mem´ non)
[3] (troi)

fighting along with countless other Greeks in a bloody war. Many women of Mycenae had to face the horrible news of their husbands' deaths. But now Clytemnestra would soon see her husband again. And the signal she'd awaited for so long meant Agamemnon was not only alive but victorious.

Clytemnestra had everything planned for Agamemnon's return. She would crowd the street with cheering subjects. Then when her husband reached the palace, she'd greet him warmly and lead him inside. He'd be tired and dusty from the road, so she'd take him straight to a soothing bath.

And then when her husband was relaxed, she'd take the ax which she'd hidden by the bath and bury it in his skull!

Why did Clytemnestra want to kill her husband? Why did she hate him? The answer lay buried in something that happened ten years earlier, at the beginning of the Trojan War.

That war started when a prince of Troy eloped with Helen, the wife of Menelaus.[4] So Menelaus and his older brother Agamemnon joined all the leaders of Greece in a war against the city of Troy. Their goal was to get Helen back and punish the Trojans.

Leading a fleet of ships crammed with warriors, Agamemnon set sail for Troy. On the way, they stopped at a Greek port to hunt for food. There Agamemnon killed a **sacred** deer by mistake. This angered Artemis,[5] the goddess of the hunt. She caused the winds to stop blowing. Without wind, Agamemnon's ships could not sail on to Troy.

Agamemnon asked the advice of Calchas, a soothsayer.[6] Calchas explained, "The winds will not blow again until you offer a sacrifice to Artemis. No ordinary animal sacrifice will do. To **appease** Artemis, you must kill your oldest daughter, Iphigenia."[7]

Agamemnon's heart broke at the thought of killing his daughter. But as the subject of the gods, wasn't he obliged to obey them? Other less noble thoughts also crossed the king's

[4] (men e lā′ us)
[5] (ar′ te mis)
[6] (kal′ kas) A soothsayer is a person who tells the future.
[7] (if i jē nī′ a)

mind. He was tempted by the glory of being general of all the Greek forces. So in the end, the king arranged for the sacrifice to take place.

The plan involved some trickery. First, Agamemnon sent a messenger back to his palace in Mycenae. Under orders from Agamemnon, the messenger lied and said that a great hero wanted to marry Iphigenia. The wedding was to take place immediately.

In a flurry of excitement, Clytemnestra and her lovely daughter hurried to join Agamemnon. However, what awaited mother and daughter was not a marriage celebration but a nightmare!

Agamemnon ordered Iphigenia to be placed on top of an altar. Then he raised a knife over her body. After saying a prayer to Artemis, Agamemnon let the knife fall. Screaming with horror, Clytemnestra watched as Agamemnon **slew** her daughter.

Instantly the winds began to blow with powerful force. Agamemnon, knowing that his men were eager to sail for Troy, spoke briefly to his wife. In a cold voice, he said, "Go back to Mycenae and wait for my return."

So Clytemnestra did exactly that. She waited for ten years until the end of the Trojan War. Now, finally, she would have her revenge. She would kill the man who'd murdered her daughter.

As she stared at the light in the distance, Clytemnestra's green eyes glowed. She joyously squeezed the hand of the man standing beside her. "Soon we'll give my husband the welcome he deserves," she told him.

The man she was speaking to was Aegisthus,[8] her lover. He'd been living in the palace with her for several years.

Aegisthus had his own reasons for wanting Agamemnon to die. Agamemnon's father, Atreus, and Aegisthus' father, Thyestes,[9] were brothers. For years the two brothers **feuded** over a woman.

[8] (ē jis´ thus)
[9] (ā´ trūs *or* ā´ trē us) (thī´ es tēz)

Then one day Atreus invited Thyestes to a feast. Thyestes was surprised when his brother received him with much affection. He actually began to enjoy himself and ate heartily of the many dishes Atreus offered.

Afterwards Thyestes nearly went insane from horror when he learned the truth about that meal. The food he'd eaten had been the bodies of his own sons! Atreus had hacked Thyestes' sons to bits and cooked them for the feast.

All this had happened before Aegisthus was born. But he grew up knowing what had happened to his brothers. Hatred for his uncle's family burned deep inside him. And he dreamt of getting revenge.

Now Clytemnestra and Aegisthus eagerly awaited Agamemnon's return. They could hardly wait to see him—and kill him.

It seemed that everyone was **conspiring** against Agamemnon. But at least one person was concerned for the king: his daughter, Electra.[10]

Electra had never really gotten over the death of Iphigenia, her older sister. But it was hard for her to feel bitter toward Agamemnon.

"My father had a reason for what he did," she decided. "The gods demanded my sister's death. And as leader of the army, my father was forced to do whatever was necessary in order for his men to win. Yet, though his duty was clear, I know it wasn't an easy choice for him. He did love Iphigenia.

"Now my father is coming home," Electra thought. "What will happen when he arrives?"

Though she was only sixteen years old, Electra was already a good judge of character. She'd disliked Aegisthus from the moment she met him. Moreover, she was certain that this man and her mother were planning something evil.

But what plan had they brewed? And how could she hope to stop them? It seemed that she could rely only on her brother Orestes.[11] And a ten-year-old boy couldn't be of much help.

[10](e lek´ tra)
[11](ō res´ tēz)

Miles away at Troy, Agamemnon had no hint of the danger that awaited him. He and his warriors were simply anxious to return home and receive their heroes' welcome.

Shielding his eyes from the sun, Agamemnon stared at the temple on a nearby hilltop. The Greek leader was a giant of a man. A brown beard streaked with traces of gray framed his rugged face.

Suddenly Cassandra,[12] a princess of Troy, stepped out of the temple. Her graceful figure and large dark eyes gave her a **haunting** beauty.

Like all other Trojans, Cassandra was now a prisoner of war. But she was no ordinary prisoner—she was Agamemnon's lover. And she had given birth to the Greek king's twin sons, Teledamus and Pelops.[13]

Cassandra was extraordinary for other reasons. She possessed the ability to predict the future. Yet she was also cursed because no one ever believed her predictions.

So Cassandra had known that Troy would be crushed by the Greeks. And now she knew what dark path stretched before her.

Cassandra walked slowly towards Agamemnon. When she joined him, she didn't meet his eye. Neither did she speak.

"My love, my Cassandra," whispered Agamemnon. "Come with me to Mycenae. You will be treated with kindness."

Still Cassandra made no reply. But pale as a ghost, she courageously stepped aboard Agamemnon's ship. Her two sons followed her.

Agamemnon thought that Cassandra's dark mood was caused by her grief for the fallen Troy. Eager to take her away from her ruined homeland, he ordered his men to set sail.

The voyage home was **tempestuous.** Storm after storm rocked the ships. Many sank or were lost. But Agamemnon's ship stayed on course.

At last the vessel reached Mycenae. Agamemnon and his

[12](ka san´ dra)
[13](tē led´ a mas) (pē´ lops)

crew were greeted by a crowd of cheering people. Waving and smiling to his subjects, Agamemnon stepped into his waiting chariot. Then the king motioned to Cassandra. The Trojan princess and her twin sons joined him.

Watching from outside the palace, a group of Mycenaen elders[14] waited to greet their king. These men wore smiles on their faces but carried fear in their hearts. They knew that Clytemnestra hated her husband for killing Iphigenia. They also knew that the queen had taken a lover. Worst of all, this lover also hated the king.

As the chariot stopped in front of the palace, royal servants unrolled a purple cloth. With respect and admiration, the elders chanted a poem to welcome the victorious Agamemnon.

Overcome with emotion, Agamemnon stepped down from the chariot. He dropped to his knees and kissed the ground. "My beloved Mycenae," said Agamemnon. "How I have longed for this day!"

Suddenly Clytemnestra appeared in the palace doorway. Smiling, the queen threw out her arms in welcome. "My husband! You are home at last!" she cried. Quickly Clytemnestra went to her husband's side and kissed him.

"So many years, Agamemnon! I have longed for your return every hour of every endless day," she declared, her eyes gleaming. "You are like water to a **parched** throat."

"I welcome your kindness, my queen," said Agamemnon. "But such praise is best saved for the gods."

At the king's speech, many in the crowd glanced at each other. Agamemnon's tone had been cold and distant.

Agamemnon turned to help Cassandra and the twins from the chariot.

"This is Cassandra, princess of Troy," Agamemnon explained to Clytemnestra. "She was given to me as a reward for victory. I hope you will welcome her to the palace and treat her with respect and kindness."

As Clytemnestra stared at Cassandra, a wave of tension

[14]Elders were advisors to the king.

passed through the onlooking elders. They whispered among themselves, wondering what the queen would do.

Still smiling, Clytemnestra bowed to Cassandra. To Agamemnon, the queen said, "I will treat her as I treat you, dear husband."

More whispering passed through the crowd. Surely this meant something evil. The smile on the queen's face didn't fool these old men. What did she have planned? How could they warn Agamemnon?

Clytemnestra took Agamemnon's arm. "You must be weary. Come with me. I've prepared a feast for you. But first you shall enjoy a bath."

Then Clytemnestra pointed to the purple cloth she'd spread for Agamemnon. "Walk on this cloth, my husband. I would not have your feet touch the common dirt."

But Agamemnon drew back. "Such pride isn't proper," he protested. "Only a god should be honored in this way."

Clytemnestra laughed. "Or one of the gods' favorites," she argued. "Surely the gods wouldn't deny you—the victor of Troy—this right."

Agamemnon still hesitated. But Clytemnestra's words appealed to his pride.

Agamemnon ended up **compromising.** He removed his sandals before stepping onto the cloth, hoping this showed some **humility.**

Clytemnestra led him into the palace. But before she shut the doors, she turned to Cassandra. "Won't you enter?" the queen asked. However, Cassandra remained frozen to the spot.

As the doors closed, the Trojan princess cried out, "By all the gods, let this end quickly!"

Hearing this, the elders crowded around the young princess. "What do you mean?" they demanded.

"I've seen this in my dreams. Over and over. The bull killed by the cow. Death in the water!" Cassandra wailed. "And then the circle of blood closes over my head!"

"Woman, talk sense!" one of the elders demanded.

"Sense? What sense is there in any of this? It's the gods' will. It's their will that I—"

Cassandra broke off and stared at the palace. A sudden calmness seemed to settle on her. "Very well, then. It's time. I pray only that the gods send someone to take blood for my blood."

With that, the Trojan princess slowly approached the palace doors.

Inside the palace, Clytemnestra led Agamemnon to a bath. As he relaxed his sore muscles in the water, Clytemnestra rubbed his back and whispered loving words in his ear.

Looking over her shoulder, Clytemnestra saw Aegisthus hidden behind a pillar. The two lovers exchanged a look of **malicious** delight.

Clytemnestra continued to rub her husband's weary body. At last Agamemnon stood up. As he stepped out of the bath, the king noticed an ax lying nearby. When he picked up the weapon, Clytemnestra gasped.

"This is a strange place to keep an ax," said Agamemnon, swinging it playfully.

For a moment, Clytemnestra stared at him, not knowing what to say. Then she said, "Please put that down. You're scaring me."

Agamemnon glanced at her. Then with a shrug, he laid the ax on the floor. "So tell me," he said. "Why is it here?"

Unable to think of a reply, Clytemnestra picked up the large robe she'd made for the king. Hoping to **distract** him, she said, "I have a feast waiting for you. It's probably getting cold. Aren't you hungry, my love?"

"Oh, yes," he replied. "Hungry enough to eat ten meals."

Suddenly Clytemnestra threw the robe over Agamemnon's head. He struggled to find the holes for his head and arms. But there were no such holes. The more the king struggled, the more he became **entangled** in the robe.

"Woman!" he yelled. "What kind of robe is this? Where are the sleeves and the neck?"

Outside the palace, Cassandra and the elders could hear Agamemnon's angry shouts.

"She has thrown the trick robe over his head," said Cassandra, heading toward the palace. "Now comes—"

She broke off. Before the elders could stop her, she'd run inside the palace. But they were able to stop her sons when they tried to follow. The elders grabbed the boys and held them tight. Though the frightened twins begged to join their mother, the elders gripped them firmly.

Inside the palace, Agamemnon still struggled to get out of the trick robe. Clytemnestra picked up the ax and raised it high over her head. Her face was purple with hatred and rage.

"You killed my daughter," Clytemnestra snarled. "And yet you really expected me to welcome you back with loving arms? Well, here are my **arms,** you fool!"

With that, Clytemnestra swung the ax, striking Agamemnon in the head. At once the king crumpled to the floor in a heap.

For a moment, Clytemnestra stared at her husband's body. Then slowly she approached the king. Her husband's blood had splattered her face. Now she wiped this blood on the king's hair, which showed through the new cut in the robe. This act **signified** that Agamemnon had brought about his own death. It also meant that Clytemnestra would take no blame.

A sound behind the queen drew her attention. With the ax still in her hand, the queen spun around. There stood Cassandra.

The princess didn't draw back when Clytemnestra started towards her. She had seen her fate too many times to protest.

But then something happened that Cassandra had never seen in her dreams. With his last ounce of strength, Agamemnon reached out to stop his wife.

However, his efforts were in vain. In the next instant, the king fell back to the floor and died.

In her final moment, Cassandra felt a surge of love for Agamemnon. "He died trying to save me," she thought. The Trojan princess smiled as the ax fell upon her own head.

With both murders done, Clytemnestra let the ax fall to the ground. After so many years, at last it was over!

Little did the queen guess that the long family tragedy was to continue. Unknown to her, Electra had hidden in a corner of the room and witnessed the **grisly** murders. The girl's worst fears were **confirmed.** Grief and hatred had driven her mother mad. And Aegisthus was worse than mad. He'd stop at nothing to become king of Mycenae.

Fighting back tears of sorrow and anger, Electra ran to Orestes' room. She calmed the boy and quickly wrapped him in a large, ragged robe. Then she pulled a hood over her own head to disguise herself. Finally she placed Orestes over her shoulder. Looking like a peasant carrying a bundle of rags, she left the palace by a back door.

Electra had correctly guessed Aegisthus' plans. He'd secretly brought his own men into the palace. After a brief, furious fight, his men slaughtered the guards. Then Aegisthus ran to Orestes' room.

But it was empty. Aegisthus growled in rage and raced off to find the young **heir** to the throne.

As Aegisthus ran outside the palace, he saw Cassandra's twin sons. At once he darted toward them. Though the boys cried out for mercy, the queen's lover murdered them both.

At that ghastly moment, Clytemnestra joined Aegisthus on the palace steps. Raising her hands, she silenced the elders and the gathering crowd of Mycenaens.

"Hear me, my people!" Clytemnestra shouted. "My husband is dead, struck down by my own hands."

A loud cry of grief passed through the crowd. Again Clytemnestra raised her hands for silence.

"I am not a murderer," she explained. "I am an **executioner.** Years ago, Agamemnon brutally murdered our daughter, Iphigenia. Now justice has been served. I declare this a day for celebration—a day to remember in the years to come."

Satisfied that she had said all she needed to, Clytemnestra returned to the palace. Aegisthus followed her. They left the stunned crowd to whisper and weep silent tears.

That evening, Electra returned to the palace alone. She had safely delivered Orestes to some shepherds. She'd instructed them to take the boy to her uncle, King Strophius[15]

[15](strō´ fi us)

of Phocis.[16] Electra knew the king would take care of his nephew.

Entering the palace, Electra gave Aegisthus an **insolent** smile. Aegisthus immediately knew that he'd been tricked. Burning with rage, Aegisthus slapped the girl. He wanted to kill her, but he knew Clytemnestra wouldn't stand for it.

So began years of punishment for Electra. Aegisthus did everything he could to make her life miserable. He refused to let Electra live in the palace. Instead, she was forced to make her home in a tiny shack outside the palace. For her meals, she had only leftover scraps.

Clytemnestra did nothing to stop Aegisthus. In fact, she sometimes encouraged his treatment of Electra. The queen knew her daughter hated her for killing Agamemnon. Clytemnestra vowed that no one would make her feel guilty for taking the revenge that was rightfully hers.

Both the queen and her lover overlooked the fact that others might burn with the desire for revenge. For Electra had no intention of letting her father's murder go unpunished. Indeed, the thought of revenge was the only thing that gave her comfort.

Every day, every hour that passed brought the time of Orestes' return closer. When that day came, Electra's wish would be carried out. Then the palace of Mycenae would again run with blood.

[16](fō´ sis)

INSIGHTS

The most famous version of this myth was written by the Greek playwright Aeschylus. Though Aeschylus wrote over ninety plays, only seven have survived.

How Aeschylus died is a well-known Greek legend. It is said that an eagle carrying a turtle flew over him. The eagle was looking for a way to crack the turtle's shell and eat its catch. Thinking Aeschylus' bald head was a rock, the eagle thought it had found the perfect place to drop the turtle.

Unfortunately for Aeschylus, the eagle's aim was good. The turtle hit squarely and killed the playwright. And unfortunately for the eagle, the turtle's shell remained unbroken.

Agamemnon's family was said to be cursed. This curse was put on the family as a result of an ancestor named Tantalus. Tantalus killed his son Pelops and tried to serve the body to the gods for dinner.

But the Olympians were aware of the trick and sentenced Tantalus to Hades for his crime. There he would starve forever, with food and water almost—but not quite—within reach. (Today *tantalize* means "to tease" or "give false hope.")

Then the gods brought Pelops back to life. This was unfortunate in a way, for the tragic curse continued when Pelops fathered two sons, Thyestes and Atreus. As this myth tells, the two brothers fought over a woman. And a second ghastly meal followed when Atreus killed Thyestes' children and served them to Thyestes.

Paris and Helen's love ended up destroying Troy. Another unhappy love affair helped seal the fate of the Trojans. This romance began when the god Apollo fell in love with Cassandra. As a sign of his affection, Apollo gave Cassandra the gift of being able to foretell the future.

But when Cassandra rejected the god, he cursed his gift. Cassandra was still able to tell the future, but no one would believe her predictions.

"Pride goeth before a fall." That saying certainly applies to this myth and the next, where hubris comes into play. The Greeks defined *hubris* as a kind of pride in which people considered themselves above the law. As a result, they tended to disregard the rights of others.

In Greek myths hubris often involved going against the gods' wishes. But generally the gods saw to it that someone with hubris received his or her share of bad luck. (As you'll find in the next myth, Clytemnestra will pay dearly for her act of hubris.)

The prophet Calchas—who told Agamemnon to sacrifice his daughter—was an excellent soothsayer. He was very proud of his power. In fact, he was a little too proud. When another prophet proved to be more skillful, Calchas died of grief.

Human sacrifice was never really a commonplace event in ancient Greece. But it did occur. In times of great need, people offered other humans to the gods in the hope that things would change for the better. Though sacrifice victims were sometimes citizens, they were more often captives of war.

Gradually—and probably to everyone's relief—human sacrifice was totally replaced by animal sacrifice.

ORESTES

VOCABULARY PREVIEW

Below is a list of words that appear in the story. Read the list and get to know the words before you start the story.

acquit—declare innocent; set free
avenge—get revenge for; punish; settle a score
defiance—boldness; daring
dilemma—difficult choice; problem
gnarled—knotted and twisted
harbor—hold onto; keep
hounded—chased after; pursued nonstop
incessant—unending; continual
justification—reason; excuse
matricide—murder of a mother by her child
morbid—depressing; gloomy; horrifying
ordeal—trying experience
peers—equals; persons of the same background or status
prosecute—bring legal action against
scrutinized—studied carefully
shrine—holy place; temple
shunned—avoided
smuggled—sneaked in or out
talons—claws
urn—vase used to hold someone's ashes

Orestes

Orestes is trapped. To right an old wrong, he must commit yet another wrong. But there may be a way out of the circle of violence—if the gods can help him both recover the past and bury it.

*O*restes[1] sat at the window and stared at the thin, pale moon. Like a polished knife, it seemed to cut through the peaceful night.

Orestes shook himself. Such **morbid** thoughts often haunted him at night.

It had been eight years since he'd come to live in Phocis with his uncle, King Strophius.[2] The king had grown to love Orestes as much as he loved his own son, Pylades.[3] And Pylades and Orestes thought of each other as brothers.

Yet Orestes couldn't put his past behind him. For with the night came thoughts of his father and mother, King Agamemnon and Queen Clytemnestra.[4]

[1] (ō res´ tēz)
[2] (fō´ sis) (strō´ fi us)
[3] (pil ā´ dēz *or* pil´ a dēz)
[4] (ag a mem´ non) (klī tem nes´ tra)

Orestes hadn't been home to Mycenae since the day his father returned from the Trojan War.[5] And when Agamemnon reached home, he found a nightmare waiting for him. For ten endless years his wife had waited to take revenge against him for the death of their daughter. Agamemnon had killed the girl in order to lift a curse against his army. So when Agamemnon reached home after the war, Clytemnestra murdered him.

Orestes would have been murdered too if his other sister, Electra,[6] hadn't **smuggled** him to safety. Since that time, Orestes had lived in Phocis. Meanwhile, his mother and her lover ruled Agamemnon's kingdom.

As a loyal son, Orestes knew what his duty was. He must **avenge** his father's death. But that meant killing his mother!

"Why can't I just forget about my family?" Orestes wondered. He wanted to bury these painful memories.

Yet every night, Orestes struggled with his **dilemma.** By the time sleep finally overtook him, his mind was filled with worry. As a result, he had the same nightmare again and again. In this dream, Orestes saw the face of a rugged warrior.

"Orestes, you must return to Mycenae and avenge me," the warrior commanded in a deep voice. In his heart, Orestes knew that this warrior was the ghost of his father, Agamemnon.

Often the nightmare ended with an ax blade smashing into Agamemnon's skull. Orestes would wake up with his heart galloping.

Finally the problem grew unbearable. Orestes turned to his uncle for advice. "What should I do, Uncle?" he asked. "If I don't act, I shall fail my father. But if I do act, I'll be guilty of a horrible crime."

The friendly king's sparkling eyes grew very serious. "I can't decide for you—nor can any other mortal,"

[5] (mī sē´ nē) (trō´ jan) The Trojan War was fought between the Greeks and Trojans. It began when Paris of Troy ran off with Helen, the wife of a Greek leader. The Greeks finally won the ten-year conflict.
[6] (e lek´ tra)

said Strophius. "For such a difficult question, you must go to Apollo's[7] temple at Delphi.[8] Apollo is the god of reason. Surely he'll be able to tell you what you must do."

Orestes at once knew that Strophius was right. So with his friend Pylades, he set out for Delphi.

The two cousins reached the city of Delphi without problems. They soon spotted the famous temple, which sat on the slope of a beautiful mountain. Immediately they climbed towards the **shrine.**

As they neared the temple, the cousins' excitement began to turn to fear. They grew even more frightened as they entered the grand hallway of the temple. Slowly they walked to the three-legged stool in the center of the main room.

Suddenly the oracle[9] of Delphi stepped out of the shadows and sat on the stool. Orestes stared at the woman for a moment, then bowed his head.

"I came for advice from Apollo," said Orestes. "I am—"

"I know who you are," said the oracle, in a voice much too low for a woman.

Pylades whispered, "Apollo speaks through her. That's why her voice is so strange."

Orestes took a shaky breath and continued. "I am told that a son must avenge the murder of his father."

"That's true, Orestes," said Apollo, speaking through the oracle.

"But it was my mother who killed my father," said Orestes. "Must I then kill my own mother?"

"You must," replied the oracle.

"But wise Apollo," continued Orestes, "isn't that also a horrible crime?"

"Go to Mycenae, Orestes," said the oracle in Apollo's booming voice. "Give your father the blood that is rightfully his. If you do not, you will be **shunned** by all people. You will be rejected by all gods. Even your body will turn against you,

---

[7] (a pol´ ō)

[8] (del´ fī) Delphi was the site of Apollo's most famous temple. People often went there for advice or to have their future told.

[9] An oracle was a person who spoke to the mortals for the gods.

for you shall be filled with disease. Go now, Orestes, and kill his murderers!"

With that, the oracle disappeared into the shadows.

Slowly Orestes and Pylades backed out of the temple, afraid to take their eyes off the altar. When they reached the door, they turned and hurried down the mountain slope.

The next morning the two young men discussed what they should do. Though Orestes still felt sickened by his mission, he could no longer try to avoid it. So he and Pylades headed for Mycenae.

On the way to the palace, Orestes decided to stop at his father's tomb. There he found a group of women kneeling.

"May the gods protect our noble queen," they cried. "May her terrible dream prove to be false. Rest, great king, and leave old quarrels behind."

With that the women poured wine on the tomb, hoping to quiet Agamemnon's ghost. Then they left in a group, still buzzing with cries of concern.

But one young woman remained behind. Orestes studied her carefully. There was something strange about her appearance. Though she had a pretty face, her eyes were red and swollen. Her hair fell about her face in a **gnarled** mess.

Unobserved, Orestes drew closer to the woman. He heard her praying in a low voice. "Do not sleep, Agamemnon, until you are avenged. Do not let your queen sleep either. May the snake she dreamed of drain her of all the blood in her body. Now accept this wine in the name of your daughter, Electra."

Orestes cried out in astonishment. This woman was his sister!

Startled, Electra spun around and stared at the two young men.

"Who are you?" she asked. Orestes read both **defiance** and fear in her expression.

"My dear sister, I'm Orestes," he replied.

It was Electra's turn to exclaim. She drew Orestes closer and examined his face.

Finally she cried out, "It is you! This scar." She touched an old wound on his forehead. "You got that the day we chased a deer. You slipped and gashed your head on a sharp rock. Oh, how you cried!" Even as she spoke, tears trickled down Electra's own face.

Watching their joyful reunion, Pylades smiled. However, he knew that this would be the only happy moment of the day. The task awaiting his friend was a dark one.

At last Orestes drew away. "Your prayer, Electra—the queen still lives?"

Electra nodded. "She does. And her hateful lover, Aegisthus.[10] But our mother may not be so sure of herself as she once was. Last night, she had a dark nightmare. She dreamt that she gave birth to a snake. And when she began to nurse the child, it bit her and drew blood."

Electra continued. "She was so worried, she asked a priest what the dream meant. He told her that the spirits of the dead were angry with her. So she sent her serving women here to quiet Agamemnon's spirit."

Orestes stared off into the distance. "Her dream is going to come true. I am the snake that she nursed. And I mean to draw her blood."

Electra's eyes widened at his words. "It is as I hoped," she whispered. "I was determined that if you did not come, Orestes, I would do the deed myself."

The three slowly started towards the palace. As they walked, Orestes told Electra of his life in Phocis.

In turn, Electra spoke of the years that she had been mistreated by Aegisthus for helping Orestes escape. Neither had her mother shown Electra any mercy. In fact, the queen acted as if Electra deserved to be punished.

Hearing his sister's story, Orestes felt his anger and determination grow.

At last, her story at an end, Electra looked her brother in the eye. "I have prayed for this day ever since our father fell beneath Clytemnestra's ax. But now that you are here, Orestes, how do you plan to take revenge?"

[10](ē jis´ thus)

Orestes explained his plan to her. "Mother and Aegisthus must not know I'm here," he said. "So Pylades and I will disguise ourselves as messengers. That way they'll let us into the palace."

"Both Clytemnestra and Aegisthus are very suspicious. Especially of strangers," Electra observed. "I'm not sure they'll be willing to see you."

"They will when they hear the news I bring," Orestes replied.

At the palace, Orestes insisted that his sister wait outside. He didn't want the queen to suspect his plan.

Orestes and Pylades asked to be allowed to see Clytemnestra. "I have private news for the queen," said Orestes.

The servant looked him up and down. "And what makes you so sure your news will be of any interest to the queen?"

Orestes leaned forward and whispered something in the man's ear.

The servant exclaimed in surprise. Then he asked them to follow him.

In the palace, the two cousins waited for a time. When the queen appeared, she stared at Orestes. "My servant says you bring most interesting news, messenger. I hope you don't mean to waste my time," she coldly warned him.

At first, Orestes could only stare at the queen. Her face was just a dim memory to him. He could scarcely recognize this icy, harsh woman.

"I come from Phocis," said Orestes. "I regret to tell you that your son, Orestes, is dead. He fell from a horse and broke his neck. King Strophius sends his deepest sympathy."

As Clytemnestra listened, her face filled with relief. A heavy burden seemed to be lifted from her.

Orestes felt his own heart grow hard. Any fear that he still might **harbor** love for this woman died that moment.

Immediately, Clytemnestra sent for a servant. She ordered him to fetch Aegisthus. "He'll be glad to hear this," said the queen.

Aegisthus soon arrived. At first he wasn't convinced the

news was true. "It could be a trick," he warned Clytemnestra.

But Orestes was prepared for their doubts. He signaled Pylades, who brought forward an **urn.**

"What is this?" asked Clytemnestra.

"The ashes of your son," Orestes replied.

Aegisthus smiled at that news and seemed to relax. "Truly, messenger, you could bring us no better gift. How can we repay you?"

Orestes glared at him. "By dying, you monster!" he shouted.

Whipping out his sword, Orestes charged at Aegisthus. Before the man could speak a word, he was dead.

Then Orestes spun on Clytemnestra. "Who are you?" she cried out.

"I'm the son you showed so much grief for," Orestes declared, his voice full of rage. Raising his sword, Orestes prepared to kill Clytemnestra.

But still he hesitated. And Clytemnestra read his doubts.

"No, my son. You can't do this," she begged. "Think of how many times I held you. Of how many times I fed you, rocked you, and sang to you. I'm your mother. No matter what has happened in the past, no one can break that tie."

Orestes paused. Then he remembered the words of Apollo. This was his duty and destiny.

The sword fell, and his mother sank to the floor lifeless.

All was quiet for a moment. Then Electra entered the room. She stopped when she saw her mother's dead body. "So it is done," she said to herself.

The sound of the struggle had alerted the palace guards. Now they streamed into the room, weapons drawn.

Orestes turned and bravely faced them.

"Citizens of Mycenae," he said. "I am Orestes, son of Agamemnon. In the name of the great god Apollo, I have taken revenge for my father's death. I have slain my mother and her lover."

Stunned silence followed. The guards didn't know whether to arrest this murderer or kneel before him.

Into the silence came the roar of flapping wings. It

sounded as though a huge flock of birds was swarming around the palace. The sound grew louder and louder, and a powerful wind arose.

Suddenly three horrible creatures flew through the windows of the palace. Everyone drew back in horror when they saw the creatures. The three had the bodies of old hags but the faces of dogs, the wings of bats, and snakes for hair.

The nightmarish hags swooped down at Orestes. With their sharp **talons** they scratched his body, drawing blood. And as the creatures attacked, they screeched in **incessant,** high-pitched wails. Orestes clapped his hands over his ears. But nothing could keep out the unbearable sound—which only he could hear.

"What are these creatures?" Orestes yelled to Electra.

Electra shouted the answer several times, but Orestes couldn't hear her. Finally Electra dipped her finger in Aegisthus' blood and wrote "Furies" on the floor.

Orestes screamed when he saw her answer. In a blind panic, he charged out of the palace. But the Furies followed him, always circling his head. Pylades darted a glance at Electra and then ran after Orestes.

Orestes knew—as did Electra and Pylades—that the Furies were goddesses that tormented anyone who committed a terrible crime. And for the Furies, the crime of **matricide** was terrible indeed.

For days Orestes ran wildly from place to place. Though he was bloody and exhausted beyond bearing, the torture of the Furies drove him on. Meanwhile, Pylades hurried after his friend. Helplessly he tried to comfort Orestes.

At last Orestes made his way to Delphi again. He stumbled into the temple with Pylades and the Furies right behind him.

The oracle stood as if she were expecting them. She coolly glanced at the Furies and then turned to Orestes. And when she spoke, her voice cut through the noise.

[11](to´ ris)

"Orestes, you must go to Tauris,"[11] Apollo said, still speaking through the oracle. "There you shall find a wooden statue of the goddess Artemis.[12] Bring it back here. This deed will bring you favor with the rest of the gods. Then I, Apollo, will end your troubles."

Leaning on each other for support, the exhausted Orestes and Pylades limped out of the temple. To their surprise, the three Furies stayed inside. Rather than follow Orestes, they crowded around the oracle and began arguing.

"How dare you help him, Apollo?" they hissed. "You're interfering with our duty to punish him. How can you, a god who loves justice, try to stop us in our sacred duty?"

From outside, Orestes and Pylades heard the Furies' angry words. Glad to be free of the creatures, the two young men hurried away as quickly as they could.

Stopping only for water and food, the cousins made their way to the kingdom of Tauris. But their welcome there was anything but warm. They were quickly surrounded by the people of Tauris and tied up.

"What's the meaning of this?" asked Orestes in confusion. "Why are you treating us this way?"

A man answered, "We're taking you to the temple of Artemis. It is the law. Any stranger who sets foot on our land is sacrificed to the gods."

Orestes and Pylades gazed at one another in horror. Had they come so far only to die?

In the temple, Orestes and Pylades were taken to an altar. Helplessly they watched as a priestess approached. In her hand she carried a long knife.

Even in his terror, Orestes couldn't help noticing something odd. "Is it my imagination?" he wondered. "This priestess looks like a mirror image of my mother—only younger. And her eyes aren't cruel and hard like Clytemnestra's."

In turn, the priestess **scrutinized** Orestes. "Tell me who

---

[12](ar´ te mis) Artemis was the goddess of hunting.

you are, stranger," she commanded.

"I am Orestes, king of Mycenae," he told her. "And this is my cousin Pylades."

"Orestes of Mycenae," she said softly to herself. Then she said, "Let me hear your story, Orestes. Something tells me that your history is a remarkable one."

So Orestes told of his life. He began with the death of his father and ended with his mission to fetch the statue of Artemis.

When Orestes finished his tale, he was astonished to see the priestess' eyes gleaming with tears. He was even more surprised when she leaned over and kissed him. "Orestes, I have something to tell you," she said.

Orestes' eyes swept her face. "What is it?" he asked her hesitantly.

"I am your sister," replied the priestess. "Iphigenia."[13]

Orestes was stunned. "Now I know that I'm dead," he said. "Only in the land of Hades[14] could I expect to meet with my dead sister."

Iphigenia shook her head. "Neither one of us has yet crossed the Styx,"[15] she said.

Then as she untied Orestes and Pylades, Iphigenia explained her remarkable story. Years ago, just as Agamemnon prepared to sacrifice Iphigenia, the goddess Artemis had snatched her away to safety. In the girl's place, the goddess had left the body of a deer. But she so clouded people's eyes that they believed it was Iphigenia's body on the altar.

Since that day, Iphigenia had been a priestess for Artemis in Tauris.

"By all the gods, how could this happen?" cried Orestes. "There never needed to be any killing. Our mother and father died for no reason."

Iphigenia and Orestes hugged each other and wept.

---

[13](if i jē nī´ a)
[14](hā´ dēz) Hades was the Greek underworld of the dead.
[15](stiks) Styx was a river that the dead had to cross before entering Hades.

Though they had never met, they felt a powerful bond.

"You must escape this place," Iphigenia said to Orestes and Pylades. "I can help you."

Iphigenia went to a chest and took out a wooden statue. "This is the image of Artemis you're looking for. Now follow me, and we'll leave Tauris."

Then she led her brother and her cousin through a secret passage. Together, the three of them fled from Tauris.

After another long journey, Orestes and Pylades found themselves once again climbing the slope to Delphi. This time Iphigenia followed them.

When they reached Apollo's temple, the three met an unexpected sight. The Furies stood on the ground outside the palace, their wings still and their voices quiet. As Orestes passed them, they glared at him in anger and snorted.

Inside the temple, Orestes placed the statue of Artemis on the altar. As the oracle stepped out of the darkness, Orestes, Pylades, and Iphigenia knelt.

"I did not truly send you to Tauris for the statue," said the oracle. "My real aim was for you to find your sister. Her presence here proves that Clytemnestra had no **justification** for murdering Agamemnon."

Outside, the Furies began to move about, unable to control their anger and restlessness. Hearing the flapping of their wings, the oracle moved closer to Orestes.

"I've made an arrangement with the Furies," said the oracle. "You are to go to Athens[16] and stand trial. The Furies will **prosecute** you. The goddess Athena[17] will be your judge, and twelve Athenian citizens will serve as jury. And I, Apollo, will defend you."

"But, honorable Apollo," Orestes protested. "It was by your command that I killed my mother. And now you want me to stand trial?"

"It was by the order of Zeus himself that I advised you as I did," replied Apollo. "But even the gods have their

[16](ath´ enz)
[17](a thē´ na) Athena was the goddess of wisdom. Athens was named after her.

disagreements. Therefore, you are to be judged by a jury of your **peers.** And their decision will finally end this tragedy."

Orestes knew he had no choice but to agree.

The trial was a terrible **ordeal** for Orestes. The Furies accused him of the bloodiest of crimes. "We don't care if a god ordered him to kill his mother," they announced. "His deed cannot be excused or forgiven!"

In Orestes' defense, Apollo spoke of the duty a son has to his father. "Even Zeus expects a son to avenge his father's murder," the god objected.

"No matter," replied the Furies. "It was still his own mother that he killed. Orestes must be punished."

And so the argument went back and forth. Finally Athena called an end to the trial and asked for the jury's decision.

The members of the jury faced a difficult task. Both sides had made very strong arguments.

"Apollo has a point," said one juror. "Orestes was only avenging his father's murder."

"But remember what the Furies said," replied another jury member. "Killing one's mother—for any reason—is unforgivable."

"I agree," said another. "A mother should never have to fear her own children."

"A mother shouldn't give herself a reason to fear her children," another pointed out.

The jurors debated among themselves for hours. At last they presented themselves before Athena.

"Honorable Athena," said the jury spokesman, "I'm afraid we have a split decision. Six of us have voted that Orestes should be punished. The other six have decided he should go free."

Athena's bright eyes gleamed at the jury. "I was afraid it would come to this. Now I must cast the deciding vote. I have considered my opinion carefully. And I am convinced that Orestes was indeed following Apollo's orders. Therefore, I have decided to **acquit** him."

No sooner had Athena spoken than the Furies began screaming. "How can you do this!" they yelled. "Orestes has committed a horrible crime. You really mean to let him go free?"

Athena tried to calm the Furies. "I respect your desire to punish the wicked. But there is more to justice than punishment."

One of the Furies shook her head. "What could be more important than making the guilty pay?"

"Protecting the innocent. Shielding the weak."

The Furies murmured among themselves. Athena, seeing their hesitation, added, "One who took on such a role would be blessed by all humans."

A softer light entered the Furies' eyes. For centuries they'd **hounded** the wicked—and received mostly curses for their work. What would it be like to give gentle kindness and receive soft words of thanks?

At last they agreed. And to mark the change in their role, they turned to Orestes. "Athena has acquitted you. Now we also acquit you. From this time forward, your family will be free of its curse of violence."

Orestes fell to his knees in gratitude. And Athena congratulated the three women. "From now on," she announced, "you will be known as the Eumenides[18] —the 'Kindly Ones.' "

After the trial, Orestes, Pylades, and Iphigenia headed back for Mycenae. As the three of them neared the palace, Electra ran out to greet them. Seeing that the Furies were gone, she hugged both Orestes and Pylades in delight. But her greatest joy came when she was introduced to the sister she had long thought dead.

For the first time in twenty years, the palace of Mycenae felt the healing power of love. That night and every night thereafter, Orestes' dreams were peaceful.

[18](ū men´ i dēz)

INSIGHTS

When Orestes was acquitted, the family curse finally ended. But before Orestes was truly at peace he probably had to purify, or cleanse, himself.

The process began with the sacrifice of a pig. The victim's ghost was supposed to drink the pig's blood.

The murderer then shaved his head and left home for a year. This was supposed to throw the vengeful ghost off the scent. If the murderer didn't do this, neighbors considered him unlucky and avoided him.

As his mother's murderer, Orestes would have to go a step further—he would have to bite off a finger. In fact, there is a shrine in Arcadia where a stone finger rises from the ground. It's said that this is the place where Orestes bit off his finger.

Delphi—where Apollo's famous shrine was built—was named after the god's son Delphus. Delphi was an important city for a long time. At one period the Greeks believed that Delphi stood at the middle of the earth.

The oracle was certainly the center of the Greeks' world for receiving advice from the gods. A careful system developed to get that advice.

First a Greek would submit written questions to the priest. The priest gave the questions to the oracle, who wrote down different answers.

The oracle then placed these answers in a bowl and shook it. Finally the god Apollo made the correct answer fall out of the bowl.

One had to be careful when following the advice of the Delphic Oracle. Sometimes the words had a double meaning.

Croesus, the ruler of Lydia, discovered that fact. Croesus wanted to control more land, so he went to the oracle for advice. The oracle told Croesus that if he crossed the Halys

River, a mighty empire would be destroyed.

Delighted, Croesus set off with his army and crossed the Halys. But things didn't go as he dreamed. The Persians defeated him and stripped him of his kingdom.

Looking back, Croesus realized the oracle had never said whose empire was to be destroyed.

From the Furies we get our word *fury*. The word at first referred to a wild, raging madness in which a person was not responsible for his or her actions. Today the word's meaning has been softened. Now *fury* merely means "anger."

Athena changed the name of the Furies to fit their more kindly role. That role and name change is still reflected in our present word *euphemism*. A euphemism is a pleasant word or phrase used to describe something unpleasant.

In the myth, the god Apollo acted as Orestes' lawyer. However, in real ancient Greece, people on trial had no lawyer. They had to defend themselves.

And, of course, real juries weren't handpicked by the gods. People volunteered for jury duty by having their names placed in a box. Then names were chosen at random. Even poor citizens could take part without worry—they were given a day's pay for their efforts.

An ancient Greek trial didn't depend upon the decision of just 12 jury members. Instead, a jury consisted of 200 or more men. With so many judging the outcome, trials tended to get a bit rowdy at times.

Cases of murder were treated differently. They were usually judged by officials in a special court session.

Several poets wrote about Orestes. The versions are all different in some way. In one version, it was Clytemnestra who sent Orestes to Phocis. She hoped he would forget about

continued

the horror of his father's murder. However, Orestes met some men in Phocis who taught him that he had to take revenge for Agamemnon's death.

In other versions, Electra takes a much stronger role. According to these versions, it was Electra who convinced Orestes to take revenge on their mother. In fact, she insisted on it. Every month she wrote a letter to her brother urging him to come home and do his "duty."

When Orestes finally arrived in Mycenae, he still had doubts. But Electra prodded him on until the gruesome deed was done.

ODYSSEUS' RETURN

VOCABULARY PREVIEW

Below is a list of words that appear in the story. Read the list and get to know the words before you start the story.

advised—suggested; recommended
ambush—attack made from a hiding place; trap
chamber—bedroom; sitting room
dispelled—dissolved; broke up
diversion—distraction; entertainment; pastime
fabricated—made up; invented
feat—deed or act, usually requiring skill or courage
gore—blood
lodging—shelter; place to stay
mock—make fun of; insult
radiant—shining; brilliant
reprimanded—scolded
sheepishly—in an embarrassed manner; ashamedly
squandered—wasted; used foolishly
suitors—men who try to win the affection of a woman; admirers
taut—tight; strained; tense
transform—change; alter
treacherous—faithless; disloyal; untrue
vengeance—punishment given in return for a wrong done; revenge
wayward—straying off course; wandering

ODYSSEUS' RETURN

Imagine being a stranger in your own home. No one—not your neighbors, friends, or family—recognizes you. That's Odysseus' situation. He's been gone for twenty years and most people think he's dead. Worse yet for Odysseus, they'd rather he stayed dead.

*O*dysseus[1] woke up and looked around. He found himself lying on a beach, surrounded by a thick fog. "Where am I?" he wondered.

The last thing he remembered after the sea god Poseidon destroyed his ship was floating ashore on the island of the Phaeacians.[2] Taking pity, the kindly Phaeacians promised to sail Odysseus home to his beloved Ithaca.[3]

But this couldn't be Ithaca! How could the Phaeacians have made such a silly mistake? "Twenty years I've been

[1] (ō dis´ ūs *or* ō dis´ ē us)
[2] (pō sī´ don) (fē ā´ shanz)
[3] (ith´ a ka)

away from my homeland," thought Odysseus. "Now I'm totally lost."

Gradually Odysseus recalled falling into a deep sleep on the Phaeacian ship. They must have carried him ashore without waking him.

Luck had not been kind to the **wayward** king of Ithaca in the ten years since the end of the Trojan War.[4] Perhaps his worst mistake had been blinding Poseidon's son, the one-eyed Cyclops.[5] Ever since, Poseidon had caused many problems for Odysseus. Now after losing the rest of his ships and crew near the island of Ogygia,[6] only Odysseus remained.

As Odysseus got to his feet, he heard someone approaching. Turning, he saw a young shepherd.

"Who are you?" asked the young man.

Now Odysseus was a born liar. He loved to spin stories and tease his listeners into believing he spoke the truth. So out of habit, he **fabricated** another long tale.

But as he drew this story to an end, Odysseus was amazed to hear the shepherd laugh. The young man knew it was all a spider web!

Odysseus got an even greater shock when the young man began to change shape. A large, handsome figure appeared in his place. This wasn't a young man—or even a human! Standing before Odysseus was the goddess Athena.[7]

"You're a magnificent liar, Odysseus," said Athena. "That's one reason I like you so much. Your lies entertain me." With a wave of her hand, Athena **dispelled** the fog.

Able to see the area clearly now, Odysseus exclaimed, "I'm home! This *is* Ithaca! How can I ever thank you, Athena?"

"Don't thank me yet. Though you've returned home, there's still danger ahead," warned the goddess. "But I've

---

[4] (trō´ jan) The Trojan War was fought between Greeks and Trojans. It began when Paris of Troy ran off with Helen, the wife of a Greek leader. The Greeks finally won the ten-year conflict.

[5] (sī´ klops)

[6] (ō jij´ i a)

[7] (a thē´ na) Athena was the Greek goddess of wisdom.

come to help you."

Then Athena explained that while Odysseus had been away, over one hundred **suitors** had tried to win the hand of his wife, Penelope.[8] Odysseus' loyal wife had managed to resist being forced into a marriage. But the suitors continued to press her. And in the meantime, they stayed in Odysseus' home and **squandered** his food and possessions.

"If only I could sneak into my house and spy on everyone there," said the angry Odysseus. "Then perhaps I could plan my revenge."

"That's exactly what I had in mind," said Athena. "I'll **transform** you. You shall enter your own house as a stranger."

Odysseus agreed to the plan. And in a moment, the transformation had been made. Though a little worn and ragged by this time, Odysseus was still a striking man, with powerful shoulders and strong arms. But at the wave of Athena's hand, he changed into a bent old beggar. Wrinkles crawled over Odysseus' face, and his bright red hair turned white.

"Now you must go to the hut of your loyal servant, Eumaeus.[9] Wait there, but don't reveal your true identity," directed Athena. "Your son, Telemachus,[10] is in Sparta,[11] searching for you. I'll bring him to Eumaeus' hut as soon as possible."

With these words, Athena vanished.

Following the goddess' directions, Odysseus went to Eumaeus' hut. This old servant took care of the royal herd of pigs.

Though he had no idea that the beggar at his door was really his master, Eumaeus greeted Odysseus warmly. He invited Odysseus to join him in a simple meal. While they ate, Odysseus asked Eumaeus about his master.

"My master is the great Odysseus, a fair and wise king," said Eumaeus. The old servant sadly explained that Odysseus

[8] (pē nel´ ō pē)
[9] (ū mē´ us)
[10] (tē lem´ a kus)
[11] (spar´ ta)

had been gone for years upon years. Most now doubted whether the king would ever return.

Odysseus put a comforting hand on Eumaeus' shoulder. "I have met your master in my travels," said Odysseus. "He's alive and will return very soon." Eumaeus wanted to believe the stranger but was afraid to trust the news.

That night in Sparta, Athena appeared to Telemachus. "Hurry home," she ordered him, "but beware. The suitors plan to kill you in an **ambush.** Sneak into Ithaca and stay with Eumaeus."

Telemachus speedily did as the goddess **advised.** In no time at all, he arrived at the hut of Eumaeus. The old servant threw his arms around the young man in delight.

Odysseus watched the scene, his heart swollen with love and pride. He too longed to hug this young man who was his own son.

But Odysseus remembered the goddess' words. So when he was introduced to Telemachus, he simply shook hands.

"Please go to the palace and tell my mother I am here," Telemachus told Eumaeus. "The suitors are planning to kill me on the road, so I must sneak home in the morning." Eumaeus headed for the palace to deliver the message.

Thinking about the suitors' plot to kill his son, Odysseus silently cursed them. He looked lovingly at his son. Telemachus had the same red hair, strong arms, and bright blue eyes as his father. How Odysseus longed to reveal his identity to the boy!

Athena sensed Odysseus' aching heart. So she secretly whispered into his ear, "You may tell your son who you are. The two of you must then seek **vengeance** on the suitors."

In an instant, the goddess restored Odysseus to his true appearance. Telemachus dropped to his knees in wonder. "Who are you?" he cried.

"Small wonder that you don't recognize me," said Odysseus. "Listen to me, Telemachus. I'm your father."

"My father? But only a god can change his appearance like that," doubted Telemachus.

Embracing his son, Odysseus said, "It was Athena who

changed me. It's part of her plan to help us reclaim our home."

Realizing this was indeed his father, Telemachus hugged Odysseus and burst into tears of joy.

When his own emotions allowed him to speak, Odysseus said, "My son, I've need of your help. I must become the old beggar once more in order to spy on the suitors. I want to know whom I can trust and who is my enemy. No one can know who I am—not even your mother. Do you understand?"

"Yes, Father," replied Telemachus. "I'll do whatever you ask."

Just before Eumaeus returned, Athena again transformed Odysseus into the wrinkled beggar.

The next morning, Telemachus prepared to return to the palace. When Eumaeus was out of earshot, Odysseus said to his son, "I will come at dinnertime to beg. But beware of your emotions. You must think of me only as a beggar. Show me kindness but nothing more."

With fear in his heart, Odysseus watched Telemachus head for the palace. The "wolves" that awaited his son were hungry for blood.

But warned about the danger, Telemachus managed to avoid the ambush. The suitors saw him safely enter the palace and go to his mother's **chamber.**

Immediately they began to argue.

"How did he escape our men? Do you suppose he suspects?" one demanded.

Antinous,[12] the most evil-minded of the bunch, replied, "Don't lose your nerve now. We'll just have to try again. And once Telemachus is dead, we'll force Penelope to pick one of us. With her precious son out of the way, there'll be no one to defend her."

Eurymachus,[13] who always wore a false grin, agreed. In his smooth voice, he advised the others to be patient.

While the suitors argued, Telemachus visited his mother.

[12](an tin′ o us)
[13](ū rim′ a kus)

Penelope was overjoyed to see him.

"Telemachus," she said, hugging and kissing her son, "I'm so glad you're back. I was worried about you. I feared that perhaps...like your father..."

Telemachus heard his mother's voice break beneath her pain. Then as she had for the past twenty years, his mother found the strength to go on. "I couldn't bear to lose you too."

Listening to his mother, Telemachus wanted desperately to tell her about Odysseus. But he kept his word and said nothing.

Odysseus was impatient as well. Finally, as the sun began to sink below the horizon, he set off for the palace with Eumaeus. As they walked, they met up with Melanthius,[14] the royal goatherd. Melanthius, who hadn't been loyal to Odysseus, was bringing two goats for the suitors' dinner.

"Why, here's the dirty old pig man!" Melanthius snarled at Eumaeus. Looking at Odysseus, Melanthius said, "Looks like you've found yourself a new pig!" With that, Melanthius kicked Odysseus.

"Why do you continue to bring goats to the suitors? Have you no loyalty to Odysseus, your king?" asked Eumaeus.

Melanthius answered by spitting on Eumaeus. Then the goatherd continued down the road.

As Odysseus and Eumaeus entered the courtyard, Odysseus saw his old hunting dog, Argos.[15] The poor animal could barely lift its head. Flies buzzed around its eyes.

Weak as Argos was, he let out a happy bark when Odysseus passed by. The goddess' magic may have fooled human eyes, but not a dog's nose.

But with the long wait over, Argos had no energy left. The faithful dog died on the spot. Deeply moved, Odysseus shed a tear but quickly wiped it away before anyone noticed.

When Odysseus and Eumaeus entered the main hall, the suitors were in the middle of a huge feast. Odysseus took up his role as beggar and began moving around the table, asking

[14](mē lan´ thi us)
[15](ar´ gos)

for food.

But though the food wasn't theirs to begin with, the suitors showed no charity. They insulted Odysseus and pushed him away.

Antinous shouted, "I'll give you what you deserve!" He threw a bowl at Odysseus, hitting him in the shoulder.

Odysseus replied calmly, "My wish for you, sir, is that you not live to see your wedding day." Only Telemachus understood the full meaning of those words.

Seeing the men mistreat his father, Telemachus struggled to control his temper. In a cold voice, the young prince **reprimanded** the men for their behavior. "This beggar will be shown kindness in my house," said Telemachus.

Ignoring the prince, Antinous and some of the other men were about to throw Odysseus out of the palace. But at this moment, the young beggar Irus[16] arrived. Wanting to be the only beggar, Irus saw a chance to win the suitors' favor. Sensing that Odysseus was not welcome, Irus pushed him toward the door.

"Old man, can't you see that these gentlemen want you to leave?" Irus snapped. "Go now, or I'll give you a beating."

"You're the one who'll soon have a bloody face," replied Odysseus.

Immediately the suitors cheered the two beggars to fight. Irus moved closer to Odysseus and raised his fists. When Odysseus threw back his tattered robe and revealed rippling muscles, Irus gulped.

Not wanting to appear too strong, the disguised king hit Irus only hard enough to stun the young beggar. Then Odysseus dragged him outside and left him there. When Odysseus returned, the suitors rewarded him with food.

As the meal continued, Odysseus eagerly watched for his wife to appear. But Penelope stubbornly remained absent.

Finally as the dinner came to a close, Penelope walked into the main hall. Not wasting a second, Eurymachus raised his glass to toast the queen. The other suitors joined in.

---

[16](Ī´ rus)

Odysseus fought the desire to stare at his wife. Her beauty was as **radiant** as ever. However, lines of worry showed on her face. Sensing her sorrow, Odysseus nearly cried out her name. But he bit his tongue and kept silent.

Penelope coldly studied the suitors. "Have you dined well, gentlemen?" she asked. "I would hate to deny you anything your hearts desire. Even if that means mistreating the poor who seek shelter here." She glanced at Odysseus. Obviously her servants had told her how the old beggar had been threatened.

Antinous jumped in to protest. "Mistreating the poor? My lady, I assure you that it was all in fun."

"I do not like such games," Penelope replied. "The laughter is all on one side."

"We would never do anything to upset you, lovely lady," Eurymachus calmly stated in his smooth voice.

"You have done nothing but upset me," Penelope declared. "You continue to urge me to marry one of you. Yet I have no desire for any husband other than the noble Odysseus. You continue to feast in my hall, eating my food. Yet most women with suitors are showered with gifts."

The suitors looked at one another **sheepishly.** Odysseus had to hide a smile. Though his wife was surrounded by enemies, she still managed to shame them.

Antonius rose to his feet. "Gifts you shall have, lady," he declared. "I will heap them on you. But in turn grant me the only gift I've ever asked of you. Agree to be my wife."

The other suitors quickly added their demands that Penelope pick them.

Penelope stared them into silence. "Such a decision is not quickly made when I have so many honorable men to choose among."

Before Penelope left, she turned to Odysseus. "Welcome, old man," she said. "Have you eaten tonight?"

"Yes, my lady." Unable to trust his voice, Odysseus spoke barely above a whisper.

"If you wish anything more, please ask my son, Telemachus."

Odysseus bowed low. "I am your servant."

Penelope paused as if debating something. Then she said, "I wonder if you could ever really be anyone's servant. But perhaps you would do me a favor. Tonight I hunger for stories and news from afar. Can you offer me such a **diversion?**"

"My lady, it would be an honor," replied Odysseus with a bow.

Saying she would join him later, Penelope smiled and left the main hall. Angrier than ever at Odysseus, the suitors growled among themselves.

Eurymachus' frozen smile vanished and his voice became harsh. "You old fool!" he said to Odysseus. "We should have thrown you out earlier."

"I am ready to give you what I gave that beggar Irus," replied Odysseus. Furious, Eurymachus swung at Odysseus but missed. As angry as if he had been hit, Odysseus forced himself not to fight back. He didn't want to do anything that might spoil his plan to get even with all of the suitors. Fortunately, Eurymachus decided not to push his luck.

When darkness fell, the palace maids brought torches to light the great hall. Odysseus watched in amazement as they flirted with the suitors. No longer loyal servants, the maids had become secret lovers to the suitors.

Odysseus couldn't hold his tongue. He demanded of one of the maids, "Is this how you show your loyalty to Odysseus?"

"Get away from me, you rotten old beggar," she hissed. "You're nothing but a drunken fool!"

"And suppose Telemachus heard you say that?" Odysseus demanded. "He might trim that rattling tongue of yours."

The girl drew back in alarm and hurried away.

Finally the horrible evening drew to a close. Telemachus rose, announced that the feast had ended, and bid the suitors good night. A little surprised by Telemachus' boldness, the suitors finally decided to do as he suggested.

Alone at last with his son, Odysseus asked Telemachus to help gather all the weapons hanging on the walls. They hid two swords and shields for their own use. Then they took the rest to a storeroom.

"If someone asks why these weapons have been removed," Odysseus told Telemachus, "say they are being cleaned."

After they completed this task, Odysseus sent Telemachus to bed. Then he waited for Penelope.

She soon appeared, glowing with beauty. "Come sit and unwind your story for me," she said. "Who are you and where are you from?"

"Ask me anything else, dear lady," replied Odysseus. "If I speak of my own past, I will flood this palace with tears. But what of yourself, my lady? May I be so bold as to ask your story?"

Feeling comfortable with this strange beggar, Penelope began to talk about herself. She told of her happy marriage to Odysseus. Then she spoke of his departure and the nightmare that resulted.

"Again and again these men press me to pick one of them as my husband. But I *have* a husband—and one far better than all of them together."

"They seem fierce men, my lady," Odysseus observed. "How have you managed to refuse them for so long?"

Penelope shook her head. "For a time, their own jealousy protected me. They were too busy fighting each other to bring their power against me. But finally they united to demand that I pick one of them—any one, just so long as I made a decision.

"I held out for a while. But then an idea came to me. By seeming to agree to their terms, I might be able to put them off longer."

Odysseus leaned forward, his eyes lit with joy at his wife's spirit. "A plan. I can always smell a fine plan. What did you do, my lady?"

Penelope smiled. "I told them that Laertes,[17] my husband's father, was very old. As his daughter-in-law, it was my duty to make his burial robe. Only after doing that could I ever

[17](lā ur´ tēz)

consider marrying again."

Penelope sat back. "The fools agreed. So I began weaving the robe. But each night, I unraveled what I'd woven that day. As a result, the robe was never finished."

Penelope continued, "The trick worked for four years. Then one of the maids told the suitors about it. Now they're pressuring me even more to make up my mind."

Sighing, the queen turned her attention to the beggar and asked again about his life. Odysseus made up a story about being from Crete.[18] He claimed the great Odysseus had once been his guest. His accurate descriptions of her long-lost husband brought tears to Penelope's eyes.

Hoping to comfort his beloved wife, Odysseus said, "No need to weep, dear lady. I swear by Zeus[19] that Odysseus is on his way home."

"I wish I could believe you," said Penelope, "but I'm not so sure. Anyway, gentle stranger, I offer you **lodging** for the night. And one of my maids will wash your tired feet."

"Only if you have a maid who's kinder than the ones who insulted me tonight," said Odysseus.

"My old nurse Eurycleia[20] is full of kindness," said Penelope. "She took care of my husband from the time he was a baby."

Eurycleia quickly answered Penelope's call. She knelt at Odysseus' feet with a bowl of water.

Suddenly Odysseus remembered the scar on his leg. It was from an old wound caused by the tusk of a wild boar. Surely his old nurse would remember it. And at that very moment, Eurycleia saw the scar.

"My dear master, it's you!" Eurycleia gasped. "You're alive."

Fortunately, Athena had sent thoughts into Penelope's mind to distract her so she didn't hear the nurse.

Hoping to hide his identity a bit longer, Odysseus said,

---

[18](krēt)
[19](zūs) Zeus was the most powerful Greek god.
[20](ū ri klē´ a *or* ū ri klī´ a)

"Dear Eurycleia, you must keep my secret for now. It's important that no one knows who I am yet."

"If that's your wish, then I'll say nothing," promised the nurse. "You know you can trust me."

Odysseus smiled as Eurycleia washed his feet with great love and care.

After the nurse left, Penelope told Odysseus of her decision regarding the suitors. "I can't put my decision off much longer," she said. "Telemachus is a man. He has a right to rule in his own household. And before long, these suitors will eat up everything he owns."

She sighed deeply. "So I plan to hold an archery contest," she said. "First, I'll see which of the suitors can string my husband's bow. That will require enormous strength."

Penelope continued. "If anyone succeeds, he must also shoot an arrow through the holes in the handles of twelve axes. Telemachus will place the axes in the ground so that the handles are all in a line. My husband could easily make such a shot. The suitor who wishes to marry me must perform the same **feat.**"

"A fair challenge, my lady," said Odysseus. "But I predict that before any of those men ever string that bow, your Odysseus will return."

The next morning, the suitors gathered in the main hall for another feast. When Odysseus entered the hall, someone threw a cow's hoof at him. Telemachus yelled at the suitors to show his guest respect. Again the suitors were a little stunned that he spoke with such authority.

Before long, Penelope joined them. She called out to the suitors and held up Odysseus' bow. A few minutes before, she had wept as she held the bow and thought how another man might soon replace her beloved. Now with dry eyes and steady voice, she announced the terms of the contest.

The suitors shouted eagerly when they heard her plan. Each wanted to be first.

But Telemachus claimed the right to begin. "It's only fitting that I see if I can match my father," he explained. Taking a deep breath, he struggled to bend the two ends of the bow closer to each other. Then he tried to loop the string from one end to the other.

Three times Telemachus tried. He was about to make a fourth effort when Odysseus secretly signaled his son to stop.

"Perhaps someone with older muscles can do better," Telemachus said. "Who will be next?

The suitors lined up one by one. But one by one, they failed.

When Antinous' turn came, he confidently stepped forward. "I'll turn this feast into my own wedding celebration!" he announced. But though his face grew red and his veins bulged, Antinous could barely bend the bow.

Next Eurymachus gave it a try. Unable to bend the bow at all, he failed miserably.

Meanwhile, Odysseus sneaked out to the courtyard. There he met Eumaeus and revealed his identity to his trusted servant. Eumaeus was overjoyed and eager to help in any way.

"Eumaeus," Odysseus said, "you must lock the doors to the main hall so the suitors can't escape. Then go to Eurycleia, my old nurse. Tell her to lock the maids in their rooms."

Eumaeus promptly left to carry out his master's orders.

By the time Odysseus returned to the main hall, all the suitors had tried and failed to string the bow. Telemachus knew that Odysseus did not want Penelope to see the bloodshed to follow. So he announced the end of his contest. Penelope gratefully returned to her room, relieved that no suitor could claim her.

Eurymachus spoke out for all the suitors. "To lose Penelope is one thing. But even worse, we have proven ourselves much weaker than Odysseus!"

"Excuse me, kind prince," Odysseus said to Telemachus. "I may be old, but my strength hasn't left me. May I test the bow? I wouldn't dream of claiming your mother's hand. I'd simply like to try the challenge."

Hearing this, most of the suitors roared with laughter. But Antinous said angrily, "How dare you **mock** us, old beggar! Get out of here before I carve you like an animal!" The other suitors added their curses.

But faithful Eumaeus handed the bow to Odysseus. Ignoring the protests of the suitors, the hero grabbed the ends of the great bow. Then gritting his teeth, he bent the ends close together and looped the string. He released his grip on the bow and the string became **taut.**

Angry and embarrassed, the suitors jumped to their feet and shouted insults at Odysseus. But the hero was not to be stopped. Taking aim, he shot an arrow through all twelve holes of the ax handles. At that moment, Zeus caused a loud thunderclap.

The room fell silent as the suitors gazed at this strange beggar. Odysseus turned to face them. "Go on with your feasting, my lords. Enjoy yourselves—while you can."

The suitors sat down uneasily. They still didn't suspect the truth. But their ignorance was about to end. As Antinous took up a cup of wine, Odysseus shot him through the neck. The suitor died instantly.

"Put that bow down, you idiot! You'll pay for that carelessness!" the rest shouted.

"You fools!" Odysseus roared back. "You **treacherous** dogs! Open your blind eyes and look at me!"

The suitors stared at the warlike beggar in amazement.

"You thought I'd never return," Odysseus continued. "You've eaten my food, used my servants, and tried to take my wife! Now by Zeus and Athena, I'll take my revenge!"

Realizing the old beggar was really Odysseus, Eurymachus tried to put all the blame on the dead Antinous. In his smooth voice, Eurymachus offered Odysseus a bribe.

Odysseus glared at Eurymachus. "Not all your wealth could buy you out of this situation," he declared. Telemachus silently stepped to his father's side in support.

Eurymachus turned to the other suitors. "The numbers are on our side. Hack them to pieces with your swords!"

Eurymachus drew his own sword and charged towards Odysseus. But he'd only gone two steps when Odysseus sank an arrow into his chest.

In confusion, the rest of the suitors turned to the walls

where the weapons and armor used to hang. But of course Odysseus had removed everything. And while the suitors stumbled about, Odysseus and his son were arming themselves for battle.

Some of the suitors still had their own swords, however. So they began to mount an attack on Odysseus. But with bow still in hand, Odysseus killed suitor after suitor with his arrows. Telemachus handled his sword skillfully, proving himself to be almost as quick and strong as his father.

Unfortunately, Telemachus had not locked the storeroom door when the weapons were hidden. The disloyal goatherd Melanthius ran to the storeroom and brought spears and shields for the suitors.

The goatherd's second trip to the storeroom wasn't as successful. Eumaeus surprised him. The old servant snared Melanthius' feet in a rope and hung him upside down from the rafters.

Back in the main hall, the battle grew bloodier. When Odysseus ran out of arrows, he took up a sword and fought by his son's side. Eumaeus joined in, grabbing a sword from a dead suitor. So the king, his son, and their loyal servant attacked the remaining suitors.

The gods were on Odysseus' side too. Athena, in the form of a sparrow, flew into the main hall to watch the fighting. She used her power against the suitors, causing their spears to miss their targets.

Finally all the suitors lay dead. Though some had pleaded for mercy, Odysseus refused them all. His desire for revenge couldn't be cooled by apologies or excuses.

Now in the quiet hall, the palace minstrel and the herald[21] crept out from their hiding places. Both begged to be spared. To these two men, Odysseus showed mercy. They had served the suitors unwillingly.

It was a different matter with the disloyal maids. Odysseus ordered them to clean up the bodies and the **gore.** Afterward Telemachus took the maids outside and hanged them all.

---

[21]A minstrel is a traveling singer or poet. A herald is an official messenger.

Next in line for punishment was Melanthius. He was cut down from the rafters and dragged outside. Then Eumaeus sliced off the goatherd's nose, ears, hands, and feet. The goatherd was left to die.

That ended the bloodshed. And Odysseus finally allowed Eurycleia to tell Penelope the great news.

The old nurse hurried upstairs. "My dear lady," she breathlessly announced, "the beggar is none other than your husband, Odysseus. He and Telemachus have slain all the suitors!"

Penelope shook her head, unable to believe it. Not even the scar Eurycleia saw on Odysseus' leg convinced Penelope.

"This is some god who's tricked us," she told the old nurse as they walked downstairs.

Penelope found the beggar in the main hall. She stopped and studied him, still full of doubt.

Telemachus watched her impatiently. "Mother, this is your husband! My father! He's returned home at long last. Have you nothing to say to him?" he demanded.

"For years I've lived in fear that someone would falsely claim to be Odysseus," said the cautious Penelope.

Happy that his loyal wife was so careful, Odysseus bowed to her. "I can hardly expect you to accept an old beggar as your husband," he said.

With that, Odysseus went to take a bath. As he bathed, Athena restored him to his normal appearance. Dressed in fine clothes and looking like a king, he returned to Penelope.

"Are you convinced now, my love?" asked Odysseus with a smile.

"It could still be a trick," replied Penelope.

His patience nearing its end, Odysseus asked, "What will it take to make you believe I'm your husband?"

Penelope stared back at him. "Not bullying or tricks," she said. Then she turned to Eurycleia. "Perhaps this traveler is weary," the queen said to the nurse. "Please move my bed into the guest chamber for him. He deserves the best bed for getting rid of the suitors."

Hearing this, Odysseus lost his temper. "Have you no love for me at all, Penelope?" he shouted. "I built that bed around a living oak tree! Its trunk is one of the bedposts. If anyone cut down that oak while I was gone, I'll see him planted deeper than the roots of that tree!"

Penelope greeted Odysseus' outburst with a tearful smile. Then she threw her arms around her husband.

Odysseus drew back in confusion. "By all the gods, why are you suddenly so happy to see me?" he asked.

"My darling husband," said Penelope, "nothing has happened to the bed. What I said was just a test. Only you would know our bed was built around a living tree trunk. That was our secret. Now I'm certain you are my own Odysseus."

The king and queen held each other tightly and kissed. Telemachus, Eurycleia, and Eumaeus watched in delight.

As Penelope embraced him, Odysseus' own eyes filled with tears. He had waited twenty long years for this moment—twenty years of one misfortune after another. Now as his arms encircled his lovely wife, he felt at last that he was truly home.

INSIGHTS

Odysseus is a central character in Homer's two epics, *The Iliad* and *The Odyssey*. In *The Iliad*, Odysseus is portrayed as a clever man. But he's also dishonest and sometimes downright mean.

In *The Odyssey*, his character has changed for the better. He's still very clever and he sometimes lies. But the new Odysseus is a kinder, more moral man.

Some think that these changes mean a different person wrote *The Odyssey*. But others feel that Homer's feelings and attitudes simply changed over time.

The suitors were certainly rude to Odysseus when he was in his beggar disguise. However, most Greeks were very hospitable. They even had a saying to express their feelings about the subject: "From Zeus are all strangers and beggars." This meant that Zeus would look kindly on those who opened their home to others.

Just what could one expect as a guest? Everyone was given food and a place to sleep, of course. Guests were also given fresh clothes, and maids were available to wash their feet. Many hosts even gave visitors a gift before they left.

How did Telemachus handle the suitors during his father's absence? He managed with the help of Mentor, Odysseus' old advisor. Today *mentor* means "advisor" or "counselor."

It was Mentor who sent Telemachus to Sparta when the suitors were plotting to kill him. From this we get our meaning for the word *monitor* (a different form of the word mentor). *Monitor* refers to someone whose job it is to warn of coming danger.

Odysseus was so loyal to his wife and family that he even gave up the chance to live forever.

During his journey home, Odysseus was shipwrecked after a fierce storm. He washed up on an island where the nymph Calypso lived. (A nymph is a minor goddess.)

Calypso fell in love with the hero and refused to let him leave. She even promised him immortality if he agreed to stay with her. But Odysseus wanted only one thing—to see his family again.

Odysseus spent seven long years on this island. At last Athena took pity on him and came to his rescue. She ordered Calypso to release Odysseus.

After some grumbling, Calypso finally consented. She even had her servants build Odysseus a new ship.

For Odysseus, trouble was not quite over after he killed the evil suitors. The next day angry relatives of the suitors showed up, vowing revenge.

Odysseus and Telemachus immediately drew their swords, ready to take them on. But before any more blood was shed, Athena stepped in.

The goddess commanded in a stern voice that there would be peace in Ithaca. The frightened relatives of the suitors knew they were no match for Athena. They dropped their swords and fled.

Poseidon, the god of the ocean, was furious with the Phaeacians for bringing Odysseus back to Ithaca. So when the Phaeacians returned home, Poseidon turned their ship into stone. He also placed a ring of mountains around the island, cutting the Phaeacians off from the sea. After this outburst of anger, Poseidon finally stopped trying to punish Odysseus and his friends.

THESEUS AND ARIADNE

VOCABULARY PREVIEW

Below is a list of words that appear in the story. Read the list and get to know the words before you start the story.

attendants—servants; people who wait upon others
auburn—reddish-brown
bleak—depressing; gloomy
brittle—easily breakable
devastated—overwhelmed; stunned
eccentric—unusual; out of the ordinary
frantic—wild; out of control
immortality—ability to live forever
limbs—arms or legs
lurked—prowled; lay in wait
marauders—raiders; attackers
ominous—threatening; frightening
persistent—determined; stubborn
recoup—recover; get back
remorse—regret; sorrow
ritual—ceremony
shifted—moved from one place to another
smug—self-important; vain
sorceress—witch; female magician
woo—try to win the affection of

Theseus and Ariadne

When is stubbornness a helpful trait? In facing up to a monster, Theseus finds that being determined may be the only thing that can save his life. But when it comes to love, Theseus discovers the difference between being strong and being headstrong.

*T*heseus[1] walked slowly around the huge rock. The long-awaited day had finally come. At last he had a chance to prove he was an adult!

Theseus' mother, Aethra,[2] watched as her son sized up his challenge. "Your father had twelve men place this stone here," she told her son. "You must roll it away by yourself to get the sword and sandals hidden underneath."

With love and respect, Theseus turned to Aethra and nodded. Theseus' father, Aegeus, had left Troezen[3] before Theseus was born. The two parents made an agreement. If the

---

[1] (thē´ sē us *or* thē´ sūs)
[2] (ēth´ ra)
[3] (ē´ jus *or* ē´ jē us) (trē´ zen) Troezen is the city where Theseus was born. Theseus' grandfather was king of Troezen.

child proved to be a son, Aethra would raise him during childhood. But when the boy was strong enough to move the stone, he would be sent to his father.

Even now, Aegeus eagerly awaited his son's arrival. As king of Athens,[4] Aegeus ached to have a glorious heir to his throne.

Theseus seemed likely to fulfill his father's hopes. Throughout his childhood, he'd been schooled by his mother to be **persistent** and brave. Even as a youngster, he'd amazed everyone with his strength and skills. Now he was a tall, muscular young man. With his curly golden hair and handsome face, he looked more like a god than a man.

The moment had come. Theseus stopped circling the rock. A serious look appeared in his eyes. However, his eyes weren't focused on anything in front of him. He seemed to be staring inward, as if searching his own soul.

Aethra had seen this look many times. It was how her son summoned his courage and determination. And Theseus rarely failed when he had this look on his face.

Suddenly Theseus rammed into the rock. Hugging it with his powerful arms, he pushed at the huge stone. His muscles bulged with the strain, and sweat began to pour down his back. This wasn't going to be an easy conquest.

When the rock **shifted** a little, Theseus found a second wave of confidence. With one last burst of strength, he finally pushed away the stone. There rested the prizes his father had left him.

Breathing heavily, Theseus knelt down and brushed the dust off the old sword. Its handle was made of gold and shaped like the head of a lion. Likewise, he dusted off the leather sandals and tried them on—a perfect fit. Amazed, Theseus shot to his feet and held the sword high.

Tears filled Aethra's eyes. Proud as she was of her son, she felt saddened by the thought of his leaving.

Since the safest route to Athens was by sea, Aethra had a

[4] (ath´ enz)

boat waiting for Theseus. But she quickly discovered that he had another plan. Theseus strapped all of his supplies to his back.

"What are you doing?" his mother asked.

"I'm going to Athens by land," Theseus replied.

"But the road is filled with danger," she pleaded. "Murderers and thieves wait at every bend. It's too risky for someone traveling alone. Do you understand what I'm saying?"

Theseus' eyes filled with that same look of determination. "Yes, Mother, I understand perfectly."

"So you'll take the boat?" she asked hopefully.

"No, I'll take the road," he replied firmly.

Theseus longed to impress this father he'd never known. Moving a single rock was hardly enough to prove himself a worthy son. But a trip over the dangerous roads to Athens— well, that might impress Aegeus.

Kissing his mother good-bye, Theseus started down the road.

His journey had scarcely begun before Theseus encountered the very hairy and very ugly Periphetes.[5] Nothing pleased Periphetes more than beating travelers to death with his huge iron club.

Theseus studied Periphetes for a moment. Smiling, the young man said, "That club you have is very stylish. May I see it?"

Periphetes smiled back at Theseus. "Why, certainly," he replied. Raising the club high, the villain swung downward toward Theseus' head.

But instead of delivering a death blow, Periphetes got a surprise. Theseus caught the club with one hand and easily yanked it away.

That still didn't stop Periphetes. He attacked Theseus with his bare hands, and a violent wrestling match began. Dust from the road rose in a giant gray cloud. Finally breaking free,

[5] (per i fē´ tēz)

Theseus smashed the villain's head with the club.

Theseus barely had time to wipe the dust from his face before meeting another villain. This monster, named Procrustes,[6] delighted in tying unsuspecting travelers to an iron bed. If they were too short, he stretched them to fit. If they were too tall, he cut them down to size. Either way, the travelers died.

Procrustes stepped in front of Theseus, blocking his way. "You look tired," said the villain. "How about resting here on this soft bed?"

"You look more tired than I," said Theseus. With that, he threw Procrustes on his own bed.

Although he was fierce and muscular, Procrustes was too short for the bed. So Theseus stretched the murderer's **limbs** to make him fit. "Sleep tight," the young hero said as he continued on his way.

Many more **marauders** attacked Theseus before he reached the end of his journey. He bravely slew all of them, doing to them what they had done to others. By the time Theseus reached Athens, he was a legend. Few people knew his name, but tales of his deeds buzzed on everyone's lips.

But reaching Athens didn't mean the end of Theseus' adventures. In fact, that wonderful city held greater danger than the open roads. Unknown to Theseus, King Aegeus had married the **sorceress** Medea.[7] The clever Medea knew the true identity of the young hero—and he presented a problem for her. She and Aegeus had a son of their own: Medus.[8] Medea wanted Medus to inherit his father's throne. Obviously Theseus could ruin that plan.

So the sly queen tried to convince Aegeus that this young stranger was a threat. "Perhaps this hero will try to use his power and popularity with the people of Athens to seize your crown," she told her husband.

---

[6] (prō krus´ tēz)

[7] (mē dē´ a) Medea had used her magic to help Jason and the Argonauts capture the Golden Fleece. Later, she killed the children she had by Jason in order to get even with him for marrying another woman. Then she fled to Athens.

[8] (mē´ dus)

The king thought over Medea's warning. Finally he replied, "You may be right. Many people would like to take my throne away from me. I must be cautious."

Aegeus decided to invite the young stranger to the palace for a dinner in his honor. He wanted a chance to size up this possible threat. Medea cleverly suggested that Aegeus prepare a cup of poisoned wine for his guest—just in case.

When Theseus arrived, the aging king greeted him with courtesy. "Thanks to you, the road to Athens is now safe," said Aegeus. "My city owes you a great debt. What do you ask of me in return?"

Theseus immediately drew his sword and held it high.

The king gasped and jumped to his feet. At once two dozen nervous guards rushed to defend their king. Alarmed in turn, Theseus drew back and prepared for their attack. "Your majesty, please!" he protested. "I only wanted to ask to keep this sword."

In the uproar, few people heard Theseus' explanation. Fortunately, Aegeus was one of those who did. Peering closer at the sword, his fierce frown gave way to amazement. Then he cried out, "Wait! I know that sword! My son! This is my son, Theseus!"

In a fit of rage, Medea tried to throw the poisoned wine at Theseus. But the king knocked the cup away.

"You witch!" he shouted. "You knew his identity all along, didn't you? You wanted to kill my son! Be gone, woman! I never want to set eyes on you again."

Clever as she was, Medea knew when she was beaten. Before the day was out, she and her son left Athens, never to return.

Aegeus may have grieved in his heart about Medea's betrayal. But his subjects saw only his pride and happiness at meeting Theseus. To honor the young man, Aegeus called for a festival. The entire city of Athens celebrated for seven days. The streets came alive with dancing and parades, music and wine.

But before the feast ended, an **ominous** ship with black sails anchored in the harbor caught Theseus' attention.

"Why does that ship have black sails?" he asked his father.

Aegeus frowned, "Because black is the color of death." He explained that many years ago, King Minos of Crete[9] had forced Aegeus to sign a treaty. This treaty required Aegeus to send seven young men and seven young maidens to Crete every year.

Once there, the young Athenians were thrown, one at a time, into a giant labyrinth.[10] This maze was so complex that no one could find the way out of it.

But that wasn't the worst horror. Inside the maze **lurked** an unspeakably horrible beast, the Minotaur.[11] This beast killed and ate every one of the young Athenians.

Theseus knew the story of the Minotaur. Zeus had put a spell on Pasiphae,[12] Minos' wife. As a result, she fell in love with a bull and gave birth to the Minotaur. This hideous creature was neither human nor animal. He had a man's body and a bull's head.

"So the ship is to set sail soon?" Theseus asked.

The king frowned. "Yes. At sunrise." Aegeus turned away and angrily clenched his fists.

Theseus thought for a moment. "Then I set sail tomorrow," he announced.

"No, my son!" cried Aegeus. "Now that I have you here, I won't lose you! No one can defeat the Minotaur! Do you understand what I'm telling you?"

"Yes, Father," Theseus replied, full of his usual determination. "I understand perfectly. Now I must prepare for the journey."

For a time, Aegeus tried to argue with his son. But he finally gave in. What could he do? He realized his son had inherited his own stubbornness.

The next day, the young Athenians boarded the ship. As

[9] (mī´ nos) (krēt)
[10] A labyrinth is a maze-like building, filled with passages that twist and turn in a confusing way.
[11] (min´ ō tor)
[12] (zūs) (pa sif´ a ē)

Theseus prepared to follow, Aegeus grabbed his arm. "If you're successful, remember to replace the black sails with white ones for your return voyage. When I see them, I'll know that all is well," said the old man.

Theseus nodded. "How could I forget you, Father?" He smiled confidently and then boarded the ship.

After a slow and **bleak** voyage, the ship arrived at Crete. Guards met the ship and herded the young Athenians through the streets. On all sides stood the citizens of Crete. Shouting insults and throwing stones, they made the Athenians feel anything but welcome.

In time the victims were paraded by the royal palace. King Minos and his **attendants** watched them pass.

Theseus boldly returned the gaze of King Minos. So this was the man who so eagerly drained the blood of the Athenians! Though he dressed as richly as any king Theseus had ever seen, he was no less a villain than a road robber.

Theseus glanced scornfully at those surrounding Minos. But as his eyes fell on the figure next to the king, his anger died. What a glorious beauty she was with her gleaming **auburn** hair and bright blue eyes!

For her part, the girl seemed equally attracted by Theseus. As if hypnotized, she stared back at the handsome hero. Their eyes spoke a thousand silent words.

Suddenly Theseus darted away from his guards. Picking a flower from the royal garden, he threw it to the lovely girl. It landed perfectly in her lap. Then before the guards could attack, Theseus calmly returned to the parade of victims. As he continued down the street, he smiled back at the girl.

The girl raised the flower to her nose. Then she caught her father's angry glance. "Ariadne!"[13] he scolded.

Blushing, Ariadne's face turned as red as her hair. She glanced at her father, who was brimming with rage. Minos snarled, "He'll be the first to meet the Minotaur! Go to your chamber and stay there until I say otherwise."

"But, Father, I didn't do anything."

[13](ar i ad´ nē)

"Yes," snapped Minos, "and I'll make sure that you don't."

Back in her room, Ariadne stared out at the ocean. She had never been outside the palace in her life. Nor had she ever met a stranger. Now her heart swelled with passion. Why did her first true feelings of love have to be for an Athenian prisoner? And she didn't even know his name. The princess was torn between joy and despair.

"Didn't you hear me knocking?" Startled, Ariadne turned to see her visitor. She smiled when she saw the wrinkled face with the long beard. It was Daedalus.[14]

Daedalus was a genius—a clever inventor who worked wonders for Minos. It was Daedalus who had designed the great labyrinth. He had also created a marvelous group of talking statues. No wonder most of the royal court secretly feared this **eccentric,** brilliant man. That was fine with Daedalus—he liked to be left alone.

To Ariadne, however, Daedalus showed his friendly side. He made her magical gifts to show his affection. Tonight was no exception. The old man pulled a bright yellow mechanical bird from his cloak. With a twinkle in his eye, he wound up the toy and released it. As the bird flew around the room, Ariadne laughed in delight. But soon she fell back into silence.

"What is it that makes you so distant?" asked Daedalus.

"Nothing," Ariadne replied.

"Nothing?" the old man said with a sly smile. "Is it, perhaps, the Athenian who threw you the flower?"

"How did you know?" she asked, shocked. But before Daedalus could answer, she said, "Oh, you know everything."

"I'm just a good guesser," he said modestly.

Ariadne decided not to fight her heart any longer. In a low voice, she confessed her feelings.

She finished by adding, "So think me mad if you will, Daedalus. But I do love him. Please, help me see him—if only for a moment."

[14](dē´ da lus or ded´ a lus)

"My dear child. What good is a short moment if your beloved is soon to meet the Minotaur?"

Ariadne gazed at him. A strange light danced in her eyes. "I want to give him a small gift." She held out a ball of string.

Daedalus smiled. He understood the purpose of the string and couldn't hide his admiration.

"Come with me then," the old man said. "But be as quiet as possible."

Daedalus led Ariadne by a secret passage to the cell where the Athenians were imprisoned. At the cell door, Daedalus called out softly, "Theseus, step forward!"

Then the old man turned to Ariadne. "I'll let you talk in private," he said. Bowing playfully to her, he walked down the hall and stood watch.

Ariadne held her breath as Theseus moved close to the bars. Though she knew he was waiting for her to speak, she was unable to find words.

"Why have you come here?" Theseus asked her. "To let me look upon your sweet face and soft hair? To light this dark prison with your glowing eyes?"

Ariadne stared back at him. "No," she whispered. "I came to help you."

Then she told him about the maze, with its jumble of passageways that wrapped around each other.

"No one has ever found the way out of it. You'll be led to the center and left there," she explained.

Once inside, the unarmed Theseus would be alone with the Minotaur. Ariadne trembled as she spoke of this hideous monster—her half brother. She'd seen it only once, but she'd never forgotten the creature. "It lets out a horrible roar after killing its victims," she said.

Theseus reached out between the bars and gently touched her face. "What weapon have you brought to save me from this fate?" he asked.

Ariadne handed him the ball of string. Theseus took it from her and laughed. "What am I to do?" he asked. "Use this to tie up the beast?"

"Let the string unravel as you're led into the maze," she

told him. "Then you can follow it back to the entrance."

This truly impressed Theseus, and he looked at the young girl with a new respect. "You're as clever as you are beautiful," he said. "After I slay the Minotaur, I'll come back to thank you in person."

"No!" cried Ariadne. "You must not try to kill the Minotaur! You'll have no sword. The Minotaur will surely kill you."

At that moment, Daedalus returned and took Ariadne's hand. "We must go now, my dear," he said softly. As the old man started to lead her away, the worried Ariadne looked back at Theseus.

"Promise me you'll try to escape the Minotaur," she pleaded.

Full of confidence, he simply smiled back at her.

The next morning, a group of guards led Theseus to the great iron door of the maze. As Minos watched with a **smug** grin, the people of Crete cheered for the young hero's certain death. Angered by this, the other prisoners cheered loudly for Theseus.

Forced to stand by her father's side, Ariadne hung her head and couldn't watch.

All became silent as the guards opened the huge door. Trembling, Theseus cried out, "No, no!"

"So much for the brave Athenians," Minos laughed.

It was a good act. Pretending to be afraid, Theseus stumbled against the door and fell to his knees. While the guards and crowd roared with laughter, he slipped the string around the bottom hinge without anyone's noticing.

Then the guards pulled Theseus to his feet. After covering his eyes with a blindfold, they led him inside. Through endless twists and turns they herded Theseus. But every step he took, he unraveled a little more of his ball of string.

Finally the guards stopped. After spinning Theseus around violently, they threw him against a wall. Then they quickly retreated before Theseus could react.

As Theseus' head cleared, he tore off his blindfold and struggled to his feet. He found himself standing in a small hall, surrounded by gray walls towering twenty feet overhead. Dozens of passageways led off in every direction. Without the string marking the way, Theseus could never have guessed which one led to freedom.

As he looked around, he saw bones and skulls lying half-buried in the slimy green mud. Obviously they'd been victims of the Minotaur. But the monster itself was nowhere to be seen.

In no mood to play hide-and-seek, Theseus yelled, "Show yourself, Minotaur! Here's one Athenian who's eager to meet you."

A loud grunt broke the silence. But from where had the sound come? It echoed back and forth confusingly. The creature could be anywhere. The dripping walls cast long shadows everywhere.

Suddenly footsteps echoed through the maze. Theseus' eyes danced quickly around the area. He stooped down and picked up a bone, hoping to use it as a weapon. After checking out three or four of the **brittle** bones, he decided they were useless.

Then Theseus heard heavy breathing. He whirled around, glancing everywhere. Still no sign of the beast!

"Is this how you kill, you coward?" Theseus cried. "By sneaking up on your victims? Why don't you step out and face me?"

Theseus' dare worked. Finally the great monster stepped out of the shadows. In that moment, Theseus knew fear for the first time.

Standing twice as tall as a man, the Minotaur had a giant bull's head with long horns. Wild black hair covered its arms and shoulders. Sharp fangs jutted from its mouth. And thick claws sprang from its hands. Worst of all, perhaps, were its eyes—cold and black as the grave.

Theseus wanted to turn and run. "But I can't do that," he thought to himself. "I can't let this thing live to kill more of my father's people. I must slay it." Theseus summoned every ounce of his courage and prepared to do battle.

At that moment, the Minotaur lowered its head and charged.

The beast moved so fast that Theseus barely had time to jump aside. He spun out of reach, landing face down in the mud.

Theseus quickly scrambled back to his feet—just as the Minotaur charged again. This time one of the monster's horns stabbed through Theseus' arm. Gasping in pain, Theseus pulled his arm free and ran to a far corner to **recoup** his strength.

There he struggled to clear his mind and come up with a plan. He thought about how the monster kept its head down and ran so quickly. "Maybe I can trick it," he thought.

An idea came to Theseus. He began running in circles around the Minotaur. As the beast spun to watch him, it became dizzy—and angry. Finally Theseus stopped and leaned back against a wall.

As the angry Minotaur charged, Theseus quickly leaped aside. The monster's horns rammed into the wall and stuck there. Though the beast strained with all its might, it couldn't free itself.

Theseus raised his fists high and crashed them down onto one of the huge horns. The blow loosened the horn, and Theseus ripped it from the Minotaur's head. Bellowing with fury, the monster slashed at Theseus with its claws.

Theseus wrestled with the beast. Finding the right moment, he plunged the broken horn into the Minotaur's heart. The monster threw back its head, let out an ear-splitting roar, and died.

Outside the crowd heard the roar. Satisfied, Minos rose from his seat. "Hear the proud cry of the Minotaur!" he shouted. "It has taken the life of another Athenian!"

At that, the citizens of Crete cheered—all except Ariadne. Believing that her new love had been killed, she couldn't even look at her father.

"There will be another sacrifice at sunset!" shouted Minos. Immediately the guards herded the remaining Athenians back to prison.

Meanwhile, Theseus followed the string through the twisted passageways of the maze. He soon found his way to the entrance and pushed open the iron door. By this time, no one remained to see him.

Wasting no time, Theseus sneaked to the prison to surprise his friends. Ariadne had told him about the secret passageway she'd used. Now he followed that path. He met with no trouble. After tackling the guard and taking the keys to the cell, Theseus soon released all his companions.

"It's time, my friends," Theseus announced. "Time to take our revenge. Let the ladies lead the way."

Laughing, the seven "maidens" pulled off their disguises. They were men! The clever trick had been Theseus' idea. Now thirteen trained warriors stood ready to carry out his plan.

Theseus and his friends quickly moved through the palace, setting fires as they went. They overcame the guards and stole their weapons. Finally they jumped from the back wall into the harbor. There the Greeks smashed holes in every ship except their own. Minos' entire royal fleet sank to the bottom of the harbor.

Then while Theseus' men readied their ship, Theseus made his way to Ariadne's chamber. Thinking that he was dead, Ariadne let out a cry of surprise when she saw him.

There was no time for small talk. "I am Theseus, Prince of Athens, heir to the throne," Theseus told Ariadne. "If there were time, lady, I would **woo** you with every lover's word in every language. But the moment forces me to cheat you of your rights. I can only say that I love you and want you to be my wife. Will you come to Athens with me?"

Ariadne hesitated for only a moment. "Yes. I'll go with you," she declared. Then grasping her lover by the hand, she fled with him out of the burning palace.

On their way to the ship, the two lovers ran straight into Minos and several soldiers. Fury and disbelief swept over the king when he saw that Theseus was still alive—and holding his daughter's hand.

"What are you doing?" Minos screamed at Ariadne. Torn between guilt and defiance, Ariadne made no answer.

The king's guards didn't wait for her reply. Immediately they attacked Theseus, only to be beaten and tossed aside by the determined hero.

The lovers charged for the beach. Together they splashed into the sea and swam to the Athenian ship.

On board, Theseus' companions were already celebrating their victory. Everyone except Ariadne cheered as they watched smoke stream from the palace. They clapped each other on the back and toasted their brave leader, Theseus.

Watching her homeland disappear into the distance, Ariadne broke into tears. She began to feel **remorse** for betraying her father and her country.

"What have I done?" she asked herself over and over.

All through the night, Theseus tried to comfort Ariadne. He told her he loved her. He said she'd be happy living in Athens as his bride. But her sorrow was too great, and she would speak to no one.

By dawn the next day, the ship reached Naxos.[15] This lovely island was a frequent resting place of Dionysus,[16] the god of the harvest. His worshippers often gathered there to hold festivals in his honor.

The Athenians went ashore to celebrate their victory. They made sacrifices to Dionysus and other gods in thanks for their safety. They also gathered food and fresh water for the voyage home.

Weary from her sleepless night, Ariadne took no part in their celebration. Still haunted by regret for betraying her father, she wandered silently along the beach.

Theseus followed her for a time but soon ran out of patience. As his anger rose, he marched down the beach after her. "I thought you came with me because you loved me," he snapped. "But it's clear now that you don't."

Ariadne wouldn't answer him or even look at him. Grieving, she lay on the sand.

"Fine, my lady," Theseus growled. "I'll leave you to your own company since you clearly don't enjoy mine."

Theseus turned away and rejoined his men. Meanwhile

[15](nak´ sos)
[16](dī o nī´ sus)

the sound of the waves calmed Ariadne. She soon fell into much-needed sleep.

A few hours later, the Athenians finished loading the ship with food and water and set sail. They'd been underway for quite some time before the men noticed something very strange. Ariadne wasn't on board!

They'd all thought she was with Theseus. But when one of the men brought his leader some wine, Ariadne hadn't been with him. She'd obviously been left on the island.

Quietly the curious men discussed their leader's odd behavior. "Why did Theseus leave her behind?" they asked each other.

"I think he never really cared for the girl," one guessed.

"Maybe he had too much wine," someone replied.

Another whispered, "Or perhaps some god put him under a spell."

Theseus kept to himself and paced back and forth. His face was like stone. No one dared speak to him. And moment by moment, the ship slipped farther away from the girl who had saved him.

Back on the island, Ariadne awakened. She walked down the shoreline to where the boat had been anchored. It was gone! Looking out to sea, she searched the horizon. But there was no sign of the ship.

Ariadne grew **frantic** with worry that her love had left her. She climbed a cliff of jagged rocks to get a better view. Though she cut her hands and feet, she took no notice. She had eyes only for the empty sea.

Again and again that day, Ariadne called out Theseus' name. But at last love gave way to bitterness. "Theseus, you traitor! You deserted me after I risked everything to help you. I hope you and your father may know as much sorrow as you have caused my father and me."

Though she'd closed her heart to Theseus, Ariadne remained on the cliff staring out to sea. As the sun went down, it lit up her glorious hair.

It was at that moment that Dionysus saw her. For an instant he thought she was the goddess Aphrodite.[17] Curious, he approached her.

Since she'd never seen a god before, Ariadne didn't know what to think. A crown of ivy circled Dionysus' head, and he carried a thyrsus[18] covered with vines. But Ariadne had eyes only for the god's beautiful face and gentle eyes. Dionysus was more handsome and graceful than any mortal man could ever be.

Joining her on the cliff, Dionysus noted Ariadne's tear-stained face. "Tell me, lovely maiden," asked the god, "what fills you with such sorrow?"

The god's kind voice reassured Ariadne. In a soft voice, she told her story, ending with how Theseus left her behind on the island. In response, Dionysus stroked her hair and spoke comforting words. He gave her magic wine which soon made her forget her sorrows.

In time Dionysus and Ariadne were married. As part of the wedding ceremony, the god presented his bride with a magnificent golden crown.

For many long years, the couple lived together happily. Their marriage was blessed by three sons.

However, Dionysus could not give his wife **immortality.** The day came when Death claimed Ariadne.

The god buried his beloved. But he was determined that something of her should live on. With a mighty toss, he threw her golden crown into the northern sky. There it burned as brightly as ever, a constant reminder of his lovely wife.

And what of Theseus? Did he find happiness too?

In time the Athenian ship neared the shores of Greece. From the palace, Aegeus spotted the ship in the distance. As it

---

[17](af ro dī′ tē) Aphrodite was the Greek goddess of beauty.
[18](thir′ sus) A thyrsus is a staff or rod.

came closer, the sight of black sails tore at the old man's heart.

"Theseus promised. My son swore that if he succeeded, he'd change the black sails to white," moaned the old king. "He's dead! My son is dead."

The **devastated** Aegeus climbed to a cliff that overlooked the sea. Overcome with grief, he leaped to his death on the sharp rocks below.

When their ship reached the shore, Theseus was told of his father's suicide. He cursed himself bitterly, "How could I have forgotten to change the black sails to white? The gods must be punishing me for leaving Ariadne behind."

But Theseus had little time for grief. With Aegeus dead, Athens needed another king. So Theseus took the throne.

As Theseus grew used to his responsibilities, he began to change. He became more serious and ruled with surprising wisdom for someone so young.

Yet the mystery remained. Why had the noble-hearted Theseus left Ariadne on the island? No one ever found out. Perhaps the hero himself didn't understand his actions. But he never forgot his love for Ariadne.

As one of his first actions as king, Theseus declared a yearly **ritual**—a celebration to honor Ariadne. "Let Athens never forget her bravery and her generous spirit," the young ruler announced.

To himself, he sadly whispered, "And let me never forget her love."

INSIGHTS

According to this myth, no one knows for certain why Theseus left Ariadne behind. But some other stories offer reasons.

One explanation is that the desertion was a plot on the part of Dionysus. Supposedly Dionysus had been in love with Ariadne for a long time. The god appeared to Theseus in a dream and ordered him to leave Ariadne on Naxos.

In another version, both Ariadne and her sister Phaedra left Crete with Theseus. Though he was grateful to Ariadne, Theseus realized he loved Phaedra more. Not wanting to face Ariadne's anger, he left her on Naxos and took Phaedra to Athens as his bride-to-be.

Dionysus—the god of wine as well as the harvest—could be cruel and frightening at times. He often drove people to a raging madness.

In fact, a group of women founded a religious group that regularly became drunkenly crazy. These women would drink until they were in a frenzy. Then they would rush through the woods screaming at the top of their lungs. In their madness they tore apart wild animals and ate their flesh.

Sometimes the crazed women went even further. They were known to kill humans who didn't show Dionysus proper respect.

Daedalus built his maze in the shape of a double ax. That's where we get the term *labyrinth*—the Greek word for "double ax."

Minos thought he had good reason for punishing Aegeus. Once Minos' son Androgeus went to visit Aegeus. Aegeus did the unthinkable. He sent his guest to slay a horrible bull—a certain death mission. Of course Androgeus was killed by the bull.

An angry Minos then invaded Athens. He threatened to destroy the city unless Aegeus signed a terrible treaty. And that's how it came to be that every year, another group of young Athenians journeyed to Crete to meet the Minotaur.

What happened on Crete after Theseus escaped?

Minos was enraged by the turn of events. He blamed Daedalus and threatened to have the inventor killed. To escape the king, Daedalus fled to Sicily. But cruel Minos followed him there.

However, Minos didn't realize that the king of Sicily had become Daedalus' friend. When Minos showed up, the king of Sicily offered him a refreshing bath. Minos didn't realize until too late that the bath was a trap. The servants poured boiling water over the king, burning him to death.

Theseus did not meet a happy end. His son Hippolytus— whose mother was the queen of the Amazons—was falsely accused of raping his own stepmother, Phaedra.

An enraged Theseus refused to believe Hippolytus' denials and forced him to leave Athens. As he set out, Hippolytus was killed by a huge monster that rose up out of the sea.

In time, the Athenians discovered that Hippolytus was innocent, and they turned in fury on their king. Blaming him for Hippolytus' death, they insisted that he leave Athens.

Theseus sadly left his kingdom to visit an old friend. But even here Theseus' bad luck followed him. The two friends got into an argument, and Theseus was thrown off a cliff.

Theseus finally did return home—after death. The Athenians forgave him and allowed his body to be brought back to Athens for burial.

ATALANTA

VOCABULARY PREVIEW

Below is a list of words that appear in the story. Read the list
and get to know the words before you start the story.

abandon—desert; leave behind
appraising—sizing up; measuring; judging
bellow—roar or howl
brawny—muscular; powerful
deflected—turned aside; changed the direction of
feisty—spirited; lively
hardy—strong; able to withstand harsh conditions
lair—den or cave in which a wild animal lives
lodged—became stuck in
midst—center; middle
murky—muddy; dark; dirty
searing—burning
seething—boiling; churning
severed—cut or sliced off
smitten—charmed; in love
solitary—single; lone; separate
sprinted—ran at great speed; raced
surged—rushed; burst forth
ventured—proceeded; went
willful—stubborn

Atalanta

You've probably heard the expression
"My heart was racing."
In this story of a proud huntress and her
admirers, you'll see that the phrase can
have more than one meaning.

*K*ing Iasius[1] turned his back on the crying infant. Normally a father would rejoice at the birth of his first child. But not Iasius. "I've been cheated," he thought, **seething** with bitterness.

It was an age of heroes, a time when kings raised sons who became legends. For months, Iasius, king of Arcadia,[2] had dreamed of having such an heir. Now on this night, a daughter had been born instead.

King Iasius asked in despair, "I wanted a son that I could be proud of. One who could do battle and sit on the throne. Of what use is a girl?"

With a heart suddenly turned cold as the night outside, Iasius made a decision. He called for a palace guard. "Take the baby into the wilderness and **abandon** her."

[1] (ī ā´ sē us)
[2] (ar kā´ di a)

Carrying the baby under his arm, the guard mounted a horse and rode off into the stormy night. He rode for several hours in the wind and rain, holding the unprotected baby. Finally, on a hilltop far from the palace, the guard laid the naked child on the muddy ground. Then he left without looking back.

Soaking wet from the rain and shivering from the cold wind, the baby cried loudly. Under such conditions, the infant would normally have died before morning. But a remarkable thing happened. A female bear heard the baby's cries. The bear gently picked up the child and took her back to a warm, dry cave.

So begins the story of a king's daughter who would, indeed, become a legend.

For over a year the bear fed and protected the girl. During this time the child grew strong and healthy.

Then one day a group of hunters passed by the cave. Their leader, Stavros,[3] stopped and turned his attention to a strange sound. He thought he heard a human child's laughter mixed with the playful snarls of bear cubs. Peering into the cave, Stavros saw a little girl wrestling with the cubs. Luckily, the mother bear was out hunting for food.

Amazed, Stavros said to his companions, "Keep watch for the mother bear while I investigate the cave."

Not wanting to frighten the child, Stavros crawled slowly toward her. The bear cubs huddled together in a corner. But the curious child stayed where she was and watched him approach.

When Stavros reached the baby, he cautiously picked her up. The girl, who had never seen a human before, kicked and screamed with all her might.

"There, there, child," whispered Stavros. "It's all right

[3] (stav´ ros)

now. I'll take care of you." But the **feisty** child yanked on Stavros' curly black beard.

Backing out of the cave, Stavros turned and showed off his treasure to the other hunters. As he held the little girl in the sunlight, her brown hair shone and her blue eyes sparkled. Despite layers of dirt—which provided her only covering—the child looked perfectly healthy.

"She seems to have been well cared for," said Stavros. "But healthy or not, it's time she had a proper home."

As he wrapped the child in a fur blanket, Stavros gazed tenderly at her. "She's a **hardy** little thing. I'll make a hunter out of her. Some day she'll be better than any of us."

The men laughed at this statement. But Stavros ignored them. He was already full of love for his new daughter.

And so it happened that Stavros took the child to his home in the woods. The hunter had lived alone since his wife died years ago. Now his house was brightened by the baby girl, whom he named Atalanta.[4] He lovingly washed, clothed, and fed her. And he taught her the secrets of the forest and the art of hunting.

As the years passed, Atalanta grew into a strong young woman. More than anything, she longed to accompany Stavros and his friends on a hunt. So she practiced shooting arrows until she rarely missed her target. And every day, she **sprinted** up and down mountain paths, training herself to run faster and faster.

One day the **willful** Atalanta insisted on going with Stavros to hunt. "I'm as good a hunter as any man," she argued.

Nodding his head, Stavros replied, "I've no doubt of that. So today you'll have your chance."

That morning, Stavros and Atalanta joined the other hunters. The men stared at the young girl. Dressed in a simple robe with her hair pulled back, Atalanta was an interesting sight. She was as tall and muscular as a man. But her face was both boyish and maidenly.

[4] (at a lan´ ta)

In a calm but determined voice, the girl announced, "I'll be hunting with you today."

The men mumbled among themselves as if they were about to protest. But Stavros put his arm around his daughter proudly and smiled back at them. No one said a word.

Not far into the woods, the hunters came upon a large buck. Sensing danger, the deer sprinted off. The hunters ran after it, straining to keep up with the animal.

Now Atalanta's training came into good use. Quickly she pushed well ahead of the other hunters. She drew close to the buck as it started to climb a hill. Seeing her chance, Atalanta stopped and fitted an arrow to her bow.

Drops of sweat poured down Atalanta's forehead and rolled into her eyes. Blinking them away, she aimed at the buck. Her heart pounded as she let the arrow fly toward the moving target.

With a loud **bellow,** the buck dropped to the ground. Atalanta stared at the beast. "Now I'm truly a hunter," she thought.

The other hunters were astounded by Atalanta's skill. They cheered her success and welcomed her into their group. Then they carried Atalanta, along with the buck, back to Stavros' home.

In the following months, Atalanta went on many more hunts. Week by week, it seemed her speed and skill continued to improve—much to the delight of her companions. They were all very proud of her. But none was more proud than Stavros.

One day, Atalanta's skill surprised even these men.

The incident began when Stavros twisted his ankle during a hunt. Stubbornly, he told the rest, "I'll wait for you here. Go on with the hunt. We've come too far to turn back empty-handed."

Atalanta was concerned about leaving her injured father alone. But she knew it was no use arguing with him. So she joined the men and continued prowling through the woods.

Before long, the hunters heard the sound of hoof beats in the distance. Climbing to a higher point, the hunters searched the landscape. Far off, they spotted two huge dust clouds. It seemed as though two animals were battling one another.

At first, no one could make out what kind of beasts they were. But with her sharp eyes, Atalanta soon saw what the creatures were. "Centaurs!"[5] she exclaimed.

Though Atalanta had never seen centaurs before, she'd heard of them. Centaurs were half man, half horse. Faster than any other creature alive, centaurs hunted everything—including humans.

Atalanta gasped when she saw that the two centaurs were heading straight for Stavros. Stavros had also seen them and was struggling to reach safety. But with his twisted ankle, he was making very slow progress.

All of the hunters except Atalanta let fly many arrows. However, the missiles fell far short of the centaurs.

Still Stavros limped on. Only a few feet more and he would reach the trees. But the centaurs were nearly upon him.

Until that moment, Atalanta had remained motionless, studying the scene. Now she raised her bow. With amazing speed, she shot two arrows. Instantly both centaurs dropped to the ground, struck through the heart.

The other hunters gazed at Atalanta in stunned silence. Then they broke into speech, all talking at once.

"What a shot! You've saved Stavros! He'd be dead if it weren't for you!" they exclaimed.

Atalanta smiled. "All that matters is that my father is safe," she replied.

So began the legend of Atalanta.

A few years later, Stavros became ill and died. After his death, Atalanta lived and hunted alone. She never complained about her **solitary** life in the woods. In fact, it took a great challenge to draw her away from it.

[5] (sen´ torz)

One challenge came in the form of a giant wild boar. It seems that King Oeneus of Calydonia had angered Artemis,[6] the goddess of the hunt. As punishment, the goddess sent the ferocious boar to destroy Calydonia.

The boar did its job thoroughly. It slaughtered entire herds of cattle and flocks of sheep. It trampled fields, orchards, and vineyards.

Not many were willing to stand up to this animal. The terrifying beast stood thirty feet high and ten feet wide. It had tusks like an elephant. Black bristles, sharp as spears, covered its back. When it grunted, steam rolled from its snout. Perhaps most frightening of all were its blood-red eyes, burning with a desire to kill.

Finally Meleager,[7] son of King Oeneus, formed a hunting party to kill the boar. But this was no ordinary hunting party. Some of the greatest heroes of Greece answered the prince's call. The group included Theseus of Athens[8] and Jason of Thessaly.[9]

Meleager was younger and less experienced than most of these **brawny,** powerful men. But the young prince had already proven himself as a hunter, so they showed him respect.

The day of the hunt arrived and Meleager summoned everyone to the palace. The prince began explaining his plan to trap the boar. However, he was soon interrupted by the sound of raised voices.

Meleager turned and found that his uncles, Plexippus[10] and Toxeus,[11] were speaking harshly to another hunter.

When Meleager called for quiet, the men stepped aside. Standing in their **midst** was Atalanta.

Plexippus and Toxeus glared at her. "Is this some kind of

---

[6] (ē´ nūs) (kal i dō´ ni a) (ar´ te mis)

[7] (mel ē ā´ jer)

[8] (thē´ sē us *or* thē´ sūs)(ath´ enz) Among his heroic deeds, Theseus killed the Minotaur, a creature that was half bull, half man.

[9] (thes´ a li) Jason was famous for leading a group of men called the Argonauts on many adventures.

[10] (pleks ip´ pus *or* plek si´ pus)

[11] (toks´ ē us *or* toks´ sūs)

joke?" snarled Toxeus.

"Does this woman think she can hunt with us?" asked Plexippus.

"I'm the equal of any man here," said Atalanta, looking directly at Meleager. "In fact, better than most."

A roar of laughter filled the air. One hunter shouted, "There's no way I'm going to hunt with any woman!" Others were quick to agree.

Meleager stared curiously at Atalanta. He'd never seen a woman like her. She had a smooth but muscular body. And her face shone with a beauty that made her seem both wild and strong.

"See how Meleager looks at her," whispered Plexippus to Toxeus. "He's **smitten.** He'll make a fool of himself."

Smiling at Atalanta, Meleager said, "Calydonia is in need of the best. I thank you for joining us."

A mixture of laughter and protest arose. Ignoring it, Atalanta smiled back at Meleager. "I promise you, I shall give Calydonia my best," she said.

"What's your name?" asked the young prince.

"Atalanta," she responded. At this, a murmur passed through the crowd. Some had heard stories connected to that name.

Though his uncles continued to object, Meleager insisted that Atalanta join them. So armed with bows and arrows, spears, and axes, they all set off in search of the boar.

Meleager led the group directly to the boar's **lair**—a large cave deep in the woods. First, the hunters stretched nets from tree to tree in the area surrounding the cave. Next, they set branches on fire and began to throw them into the cave. They hoped the smoke would drive the boar out of the cave.

Suddenly their pack of hunting dogs began to bark furiously. Standing on a rock above the others, Atalanta pointed in the distance. "There it is!" she shouted.

Meleager joined her on the rock. "Where?" he asked.

"In the swamp," Atalanta pointed. She jumped off the rock and started in that direction.

Meleager started after her, but his uncles caught him by the arm. "Let her go," said Toxeus. "Good riddance. We don't need her."

Meleager pulled away from his uncles. "But she may need me," he shot back.

"Fool!" growled Plexippus.

Paying no attention to his uncles, Meleager set off after Atalanta. He soon caught up with her as she stalked through the woods.

"Surely you don't intend to face the boar alone?" he asked.

"You and your men are welcome to join me," she replied, looking straight ahead with determination.

Meleager chuckled and said, "You're not like any woman I've ever met."

"I've rarely met other women. What are they like?" asked Atalanta curiously.

Meleager smiled and shook his head. He couldn't think of an answer to the unusual question. Atalanta smiled back at him. She liked this young man with the bright, intelligent eyes.

The pair continued toward the swamp. Soon they reached its **murky** waters. Tall, thick grass rose all around, making it hard to see more than a few feet ahead. Atalanta and Meleager waded into the water. Quietly they moved forward, brushing aside the grass.

After only a short time, they heard a loud snort. Peering through the grass ahead, Atalanta caught sight of one of the boar's big red eyes.

Wasting not a moment, Atalanta took aim with her bow and let an arrow fly. The shot promised to be good. However, the thick grass **deflected** the arrow. It ended up bouncing off the boar's tusk. The startled beast let out an ear-splitting roar.

Back at the cave, the other hunters heard the horrible sound. Theseus shouted, "Atalanta was right! The boar is in the swamp!" Immediately the men and their hunting dogs raced toward the marsh.

Meanwhile Atalanta and Meleager stood as still as statues.

"Our best chance," Atalanta whispered to Meleager, "is to sneak up on the beast."

But even as she spoke this warning, the other men and their barking dogs splashed into the swamp. "Be quiet and spread out!" Meleager hissed.

It was too late. With another roar, the boar charged. Almost immediately two men were trampled under the beast's huge feet. Two more were speared by its tusks. Water and blood splashed everywhere.

Jason hurled a misguided spear that killed one of the dogs. And worse yet, one hunter threw a spear that hit a fellow hunter. The men rushed about in confusion as the raging monster took more lives.

Even the skillful Atalanta trembled with fear. She shot many arrows but missed her mark. Finally she had just one arrow left.

"I must not fail," she thought. Carefully she fitted the arrow into her bow and aimed. Holding her breath, she released her shot.

The arrow soared through the air with lightning speed—and **lodged** firmly in the boar's throat. Atalanta was the first to wound the beast.

The boar staggered and slowed its charge. Meleager quickly crept forward and drove a spear through the animal's brain. With a thundering crash, the animal fell dead to the ground.

The relieved hunters cheered. They gathered around the boar and helped drag it out of the swamp. Then Theseus and Jason **severed** the boar's head. They offered it to Meleager as a victory prize. But he refused the head, insisting that Atalanta had earned it.

"After all, her arrow delivered the wound that wore down the monster," Meleager explained.

Plexippus and Toxeus exploded with rage. Pushing Atalanta aside, they grabbed the boar's head and began to drag it away.

Toxeus glared at Meleager. "You've made a fool of yourself," he snapped, "all because of this woman!"

It was true that Meleager already loved Atalanta. Now his uncles' rudeness to her drove him into a wild fury. He swiftly drew his sword and attacked his uncles.

Plexippus and Toxeus also drew their swords. But the prince, who was faster and more skillful than the older men, slew them with ease.

As Meleager stood over the bodies of his uncles, everyone drew back in shock. Helplessly, Meleager tried to explain. But everyone met him with cold eyes. And none were colder than Atalanta's.

Looking straight at him, she said, "So this is how you settle disagreements. Your behavior disgusts me." Without another word, she disappeared into the woods.

Meleager sank to his knees in grief. He had just killed his uncles out of love for Atalanta. But now she was gone— probably forever.

This wasn't the end of Meleager's woe. Word of the dreadful killings quickly sped to the palace. One of the first who learned of the deed was his mother, Althea.[12]

Althea sank into a chair, stunned and outraged. The sorrow she felt for her brothers was mixed with fury at her son.

"How could Meleager do such a wicked thing?" she asked herself.

In her rage, Althea took a locked box from a shelf. She quickly opened the box and removed a half-burnt log.

This was no ordinary log. Many years ago, when Meleager was a child, the three Fates[13] had visited Althea. Throwing a log on the fire, the Fates made an alarming announcement.

"When this log burns to ashes," they said, "your son's life will end."

Of course, Althea wanted to protect her young son. So she snatched the log from the fire and smothered the flame. Then she put the piece of wood in a locked box for safekeeping.

---

[12](al thē′ a)
[13]The three Fates were goddesses who determined the destiny of humans.

Now overcome with rage at her brothers' deaths, Althea built a fire. Cursing her own son, she threw the log into the flames.

Far away on a hillside, Meleager cried out as a **searing** pain tore through his body. He fell to the ground, screaming in agony.

Dry with age, Althea's log turned to ash very quickly. When every bit of wood was burned up, Meleager died.

After this hunt, Atalanta eagerly returned to her home in the mountains. Yet in time, the memory of the bloody day faded. Once more she **ventured** out into the world to seek excitement.

On one such trip, she passed through the land of Arcadia. Here a most incredible thing happened.

King Iasius had heard stories about the woman who hunted as well as any man—and better than most. When he learned she was in the area, he sent for her.

Soon a messenger brought Atalanta to the palace. When the king saw the young woman, he noticed how much she looked like his dead wife.

Suddenly Iasius realized that this young woman was his daughter. That knowledge released a wildfire of emotions. The old man had been miserable for years. Guilt over abandoning his child had almost driven him insane. Sobbing, he threw himself at Atalanta's feet.

Atalanta didn't know what to do. Why was this strange king kneeling before her and crying?

At last the king told Atalanta his story of leaving a baby in the wilderness. As Atalanta listened to this amazing story, she felt a mixture of anger and sadness. She didn't know whether to strike Iasius or hug him. This weeping old man was her father!

"To think I wanted to raise a son who would become a legend. Well, my daughter, you became a legend without me!" cried the king. "Can you ever forgive me for my foolishness?"

As she looked into Iasius' pleading eyes, Atalanta took pity on him. "I will try, Father," she replied. "But I think it will take time for both of us to feel comfortable with one another."

"Then give me that time," the king urged. "Stay here with me. You shall have the best of everything. Whatever you wish will be yours."

Atalanta accepted—but not because the king's wealth tempted her. Instead, she longed to fill the hole in her heart left by Stavros' death.

Thus began Atalanta's life as the princess of Arcadia. She happily spent her days hunting in the royal fields. King Iasius loved her very much. And in time, Atalanta returned his love.

However, father and daughter didn't always agree on everything. Iasius wanted his daughter to choose a husband. Atalanta, on the other hand, had no interest in marriage. To her, men were father figures or hunting companions, nothing more.

For months, Iasius begged his daughter to marry. "Please take a husband and give me a grandchild before I die," he pleaded.

Finally Atalanta devised a plan that would keep them both happy. "All right, Father. But I'll only marry the man who can beat me in a foot race. However, any man who challenges me and loses will be put to death."

Realizing this would be the best deal he could get from Atalanta, Iasius agreed. He hoped that as swift-footed as his daughter was, someone might be quicker still.

The king announced the challenge far and wide. Hippomenes,[14] an athlete and planner of royal games, would be the judge.

From the start, Hippomenes and Atalanta were friends. The strong, handsome man made jokes before each race. For example, he might say, "Beautiful day to get married." His remarks never failed to draw a smile from Atalanta.

Many men risked death and accepted the challenge.

[14](hi pom´ e nēz)

Atalanta's great beauty and strength caused men to fall hopelessly in love with her.

Serving as judge turned out to be a boring job for Hippomenes. He hardly needed to keep his eye on the finish line. Atalanta left all of her challengers far behind.

While Hippomenes may have been a lazy judge of the race, he couldn't help **appraising** Atalanta. Day by day, he grew more attracted to her. Finally the desperate young man went to the temple of Aphrodite,[15] goddess of love and beauty. He prayed for her help to make Atalanta his wife.

In answer to his prayer, Aphrodite herself appeared.

Hippomenes sank to his knees in wonder. "Great goddess, thank you for listening to me."

Aphrodite smiled. "Your words touched me. Besides, it's time that Atalanta showed me a little respect."

Aphrodite presented Hippomenes with a small bag. "Here's the gift to win your love," she declared. "Inside are three golden apples. Any mortal who sees these apples will feel an overwhelming desire to have them."

Then the goddess explained the rest of her plan. Hippomenes listened in delight.

"It's brilliant," Hippomenes said when she'd finished. "How can I ever thank you?"

"You've already thanked me. You could pay me no higher compliment than by falling in love."

Hippomenes returned to the palace, eager to put the plan to a test. Bright and early the next morning, he sprang his surprise on Atalanta.

"Where is the poor fool I must race today?" Atalanta asked.

Hippomenes bowed. "At your service, my lady."

"You?" Atalanta cried. "No, Hippomenes, don't be foolish. Don't throw your life away. We're friends."

"All the more reason for us to marry," replied the confident Hippomenes.

"Please, Hippomenes," Atalanta begged.

[15](af ro dī́ tē)

Hippomenes shook his head. "I'll do anything and everything to please you—after I win the race."

Seeing his determination, Atalanta offered a warning. "I won't run any slower on your account," she said.

"I don't expect you to," Hippomenes said softly.

And so a race was called. This time King Iasius himself served as judge. A larger crowd than usual surrounded the race track. Hippomenes had many friends who were eager to see him win.

Great tension filled the air as Atalanta and Hippomenes lined up together. "Beautiful day to get married," said Hippomenes with a smile.

But Atalanta couldn't smile back. The thought of winning had never filled her with less joy.

Iasius gave the signal and the race began. At first the two runners stayed side by side. But soon Hippomenes grew short of breath and his throat became dry. A burning feeling rose in his stomach. Atalanta, however, looked quite at ease, her long hair flying as she ran.

"She runs faster than a fire before the wind," Hippomenes thought. "But let's see if this will slow her down."

Taking one of the golden apples which he carried, Hippomenes threw it to the side of the track just ahead of Atalanta.

When she saw the apple, Atalanta was unable to control herself. She stopped to pick it up. And though it took her but a few moments, Hippomenes **surged** ahead of her.

Embarrassed at her foolishness, Atalanta quickly returned to the track. She soon caught up with the exhausted Hippomenes.

Once more Atalanta passed Hippomenes. And then Hippomenes took another apple and threw it to the side of the track.

Again unable to resist, Atalanta ran after the golden fruit. But as before, she soon caught up with and passed her challenger.

Not far ahead lay the finish line. Panting heavily, Hippomenes struggled to keep up his pace.

"Now is the time," Hippomenes thought. "If I wait any longer, I'll never catch her."

As Hippomenes was about to throw the last apple, he made the mistake of looking at the golden prize. Its wonderful beauty nearly stopped him cold in his tracks.

Hippomenes summoned every ounce of his willpower. "Remember what the real prize is," he told himself. Then he hurled the last apple to Atalanta's side. This time it landed farther from the track.

Atalanta was within four strides of the finish line. But the apple worked its magic. She halted to pick it up and Hippomenes stumbled ahead. With an instant to spare, he crossed the finish line just ahead of his love and sank to the ground.

The crowd went wild. Storming the field, the cheering mob swarmed around Hippomenes. They lifted him up and marched about the track.

Finally the crowd shouted itself into silence. At last Hippomenes dared to approach Atalanta.

She stared at him wordlessly for a moment. Then she declared, "You tricked me."

Hippomenes studied her lovely features. "I can't take the credit," he said with a gentle smile. "It was Aphrodite who tricked you. Only a goddess could beat the mighty Atalanta."

Atalanta started towards Hippomenes as if to attack him. But she clasped him in her arms and kissed him instead. And the surprised crowd cheered more loudly than ever.

The loudest cries of joy that day came from King Iasius. He'd never been prouder of his legendary daughter.

INSIGHTS

Some myths show that Atalanta and Hippomenes didn't live happily ever after—because they made two mistakes. First, Hippomenes was so overjoyed that he forgot to thank Aphrodite for her help. And if that wasn't enough to make Aphrodite angry, Hippomenes and Atalanta made love in the goddess' sacred temple.

The goddess didn't take this lightly. One day, as the couple were walking through the woods, Aphrodite turned them into lions.

Of course, the typical Greek marriage wasn't settled by the outcome of a foot race. Money and goods played a key role—not physical fitness or attractiveness. Often a suitor paid a certain number of oxen to the father of the girl he wished to marry. In turn, the girl's father sent off his daughter to her new husband with money, jewelry, and clothing.

By law, a formal engagement ceremony had to take place at the home of the girl's father. While witnesses were required, the bride-to-be herself didn't have to be there.

A few days later, a feast was held in the home of the girl's father. During the feast, men sat on one side of the room and women on the other. Much wine and wedding cake were served.

Finally a procession led the bride and groom to the house of the groom's parents. There the bride was welcomed into the groom's family during a religious ceremony. (However, no priest was involved in the ceremony.)

Atalanta must have been a swift runner indeed to defeat so many suitors. Most Greek men and women were trained early on in athletics—long-distance running included.

Such training wasn't merely for the purpose of sport. Fast runners were needed to deliver messages from one city to the next. These messengers were especially important during wartime. After one battle—which took place in a city called Marathon—the soldiers sent their quickest messenger to Athens to announce the Athenians' victory.

This runner traveled at top speed from Marathon to Athens. There he gasped out the news of victory and then died.

Today marathons are still held. A marathon is any race of 26 miles 385 yards—which happens to be the distance between Marathon and Athens.

The Greeks loved all sports, not just running. Athletic games were held all over Greece. The contests featured such sports as wrestling, foot racing, discus throwing, and chariot racing.

The best known of these games was the Olympics, which were originally held every four years at Olympia. The games were as important to Greeks as they are to current sports fans. Greeks from all over attended, either as athletes or onlookers. In fact, all Greek wars were postponed during the Olympics. And Greek states were heavily fined if any traveler passing through was attacked or injured during the games.

The Olympics weren't just an athletic contest. Competitions involving music and poetry also took place. The games also provided a chance for merchants to sell goods. In booths circling the stadium, they sold everything from wine and fruit to horses and pottery.

While the merchants doubtless found many benefits in attending the Olympics, athletes were more simply rewarded. For their efforts, Olympic champions received wreaths of olive leaves. Though this might not seem like much to us, athletes treasured the simple garlands.

At other, smaller athletic games more valuable prizes were given. For example a winner might receive a new shield or 100 vases of olive oil. Sometimes, too, the cities rewarded their own winning athletes with money.

GODS AND HEROES
OF GREEK AND ROMAN
MYTHOLOGY

Greek Name	Roman Name
Aphrodite	Venus
(Phoebus) Apollo	(Phoebus) Apollo
Ares	Mars, Mavors
Artemis	Diana
(Pallas) Athena	Minerva
Cronus	Saturn
Demeter	Ceres
Dionysus, Bacchus	Bacchus, Liber
Eros	Cupid
Gaea	Ge, Earth, Terra
Hades, Pluto	Pluto, Dis
Helios, Hyperion	Sol
Hephaestus	Vulcan, Mulciber
Hera	Juno
Heracles	Hercules
Hermes	Mercury
Hestia	Vesta
Odysseus	Ulysses
Persephone, Kore	Proserpina, Proserpine
Poseidon	Neptune
Rhea	Ops
Uranus	Uranus, Coelus
Zeus	Jupiter, Jove